MW01060628

"Remarkable questions answered by remarkable women. This book shows us that across differences in ages, cultures, races, and religions, we are still more alike than we are unalike. A fascinating collection!"

MAYA ANGELOU

Award-winning poet, memoirist and civil rights activist

"At a time in history when we all need hope and solidarity, this book brings to us the voices of women whose lives exude such hope. Their words of courage and love give us all the confidence to reach into our own hearts and find our own courage and love to meet the challenges of life."

MAIREAD MAGUIRE

Nobel Peace Prize winner and founder of Peace People

"Zoë Sallis has assembled a brilliantly starry line-up for her book. What's more she has elicited from them many unexpected and revealing insights, which tell us so much about how the world's most distinguished women see their lives and the lives of their less fortunate sisters. A magnificent achievement."

DAME ANN LESLIE

Award-winning journalist and broadcaster

ZOË SALLIS

VOICES OF POWERFUL WOMEN

Words of wisdom from 40 of the world's most inspiring women

This edition first published in the UK and USA in 2019 by
Watkins, an imprint of Watkins Media Limited
Unit 11, Shepperton House
89–93 Shepperton Road
London
N1 3DF

This is an updated edition of *Our Stories Our Visions*, published by Duncan Baird Publishing in 2009

enquiries@watkinspublishing.com

3 5 7 9 10 8 6 4 2

Designed and typeset by JCS Publishing Services Ltd

Printed and bound in the United Kingdom by TJ International Ltd, Padstow, Cornwall

A CIP record for this book is available from the British Library

ISBN: 978-1-78678-219-9

www.watkinspublishing.com

This book is dedicated to my grandchildren.

“The future belongs to those who believe in the beauty of their dreams.”

ELEANOR ROOSEVELT

CONTENTS

INTRODUCTION

"One isn't necessarily born with courage, but one is born with potential. Without courage, we cannot practise any other virtue with consistency. We cannot be kind, true, merciful, generous, honest."

MAYA ANGELOU

I have interviewed some extraordinary women for this book, and been deeply moved by their answers to the questions I put to them. One of the things they certainly share is courage. It was Albert Einstein who said, "The world is a dangerous place. Not because of the people who are evil, but because of the people who don't do anything about it."

All the women in this book are doing something about it, something that makes a difference. Whether they are in the public eye as activists, artists, performers, lawyers, presidents, or are simply humanitarians working behind the scenes, all of them have inspired and encouraged me in my own life. They prove again and again that the centuries of struggle to gain independence and equality for women are coming to an end, in all fields and in many countries. The great women of the past – and there have been many – had more to contend with than we do. Yet many of us still feel that it is too hard to accomplish our goals, or hesitate to act because we fear that we might fail. We forget that everything starts with a single, small step.

Professor Wangari Maathai, the first African woman to receive the Nobel Peace Prize, sometimes quoted a story about this. It is about a huge fire that broke out in a forest. All the threatened animals were scared, and fled, except the hummingbird, who decided to stay and put out the fire. It flew to the nearest river and picked up a few drops of water, then came back and put them on the fire. The other animals watched from a distance and made fun of the hummingbird. The more they mocked, the harder the hummingbird worked, persistently and patiently bringing its little drops of water to put out the fire. They asked, "What are you doing? The fire is overwhelming, how can you make a difference? You are too little anyway." The hummingbird answered, "I am doing the best I can."

Aspiration, not necessarily achievement, is what shows us the heart and mind of a person, and it can touch and move those who have the power to change things. My hope is that this book will inspire and motivate everyone who reads it, man or woman, to "do the best they can" for the human family and the world we live in.

ZOË SALLIS

DID YOUR UPBRINGING OR EARLY EXPERIENCES INFLUENCE THE DIRECTION YOUR LIFE TOOK? | 1

Jane Fonda

I think what influenced me the most was movies that my father was in. Things like *The Grapes of Wrath* and *12 Angry Men* and *Young Mr Lincoln* and *The Ox-Bow Incident*. My father was a very remote person who never spoke a lot to us, but the roles he played in these films communicated certain values to me. I once asked Martin Luther King's daughter Yolanda if her dad took her on his knee and told her about values, and she said that he never did. And I said my father didn't either, but that she had Martin Luther's sermons and I had my father's films. That's where the values came from.

Where it got to be a problem was in the '60s and '70s with the Vietnam War. I became an activist, and this generational split occurred in the family. My father wasn't Clarence Darrow, or Tom Joad or Abraham Lincoln, characters he played and aspired to be. There was a contradiction between who he actually was and who the roles portrayed him as. It was a shock to me as a young activist to realize that I was going further than he would. He would vote for a candidate that wanted to end the war, but he wouldn't march with me.

Jung Chang

My childhood was dominated by the fact that I grew up under Mao. My family life, like that of every Chinese person at the time, was completely turned upside down. This is of course one of the reasons I came to write Mao's biography, having already related our family story in my previous book, *Wild Swans*. Both books were prompted by my direct experiences.

I realize that compared to most people in China when Mao came to power, I at first had a very privileged life, as both my parents were communist officials. Therefore, I didn't really suffer much in the great famine in China between 1958 and 1961 in which nearly 40 million people died of starvation and overwork. But I certainly suffered under Mao during the ten-year period of the Cultural Revolution. My parents were denounced, resulting in my father's death. He had been tortured, and forced to burn his beloved library. My dear grandmother died and I was exiled to a bleak area of the Himalayas to work as a peasant, a "barefoot doctor", a steel worker and an electrician. Yet eventually I became one of the very few Chinese people to achieve a university education at that time. Mao had closed down the country's schools and universities for years and a whole generation of philistines was created. When he died in 1976, some limited scholarships for study abroad were awarded on an academic basis. I was in one of the first groups of 14 people allowed to come to the West to study. So although I suffered along with most Chinese people, I was also very lucky.

American Poet/Activist/memoirist/civil rights Activist.

Maya Angelou

I am sure the events I've lived through did influence the path my life took. I was raised by a grandmother, my father's mother, who was an incredible woman. Imagine at the turn of the last century a black woman in a little village in Arkansas who has gone through the 4th grade, has had her husband leave her with two children, and just teaches herself and builds up a business making chicken pies that she sells to workers in the only big places in town – a cotton gin and a lumber mill. She would cook the pies all night and carry them to the cotton gin where she fried them on a brazier, and then ran five miles to the lumber mill to sell the rest. Rain and snow didn't matter. She built up a custom like that, and in about ten years started a merchandise store between the two patronages. I loved to imitate her, and people would say, "Oh Mrs Henderson, I see you're with your shadow," and she would look at me and smile, "Yes, she must be my shadow. Where I go, she goes. Where I stop, she stops." She loved me.

"My grandmother would cook the pies all night and carry them to the cotton gin where she fried them on a brazier, and then ran five miles to the lumber mill to sell the rest. Rain and snow didn't matter."

MAYA ANGELOU

Benazir Bhutto

The direction my life took was very much influenced by my upbringing. I was fortunate to have a father who believed that a daughter and a son must have equal rights. This was not usual in Pakistan when I was growing up. Pakistan was a traditional society. Girls were expected to get married, boys were expected to get a job and look after not only themselves but other members of their family. The emphasis was on making sure that the boys got the good education – the good food. The girls basically got the leftovers. My father was different. He was an educated and emancipated man and he brought us up to believe in gender equality. Had it not been for him, perhaps I would not have been so dedicated in my commitment to women's rights and women's empowerment. It was my father who decided that he would send me abroad for education when I was 16. I became very independent when I was in the States, but at first I felt I had been thrown into the deep end of a pool, and had to swim or sink. I found it quite shocking that students went to class in jeans, often dirty jeans and a t-shirt, and would put their feet up on the desks and answer the teachers back, but it was a real awakening for me.

I was in America at a very interesting time. Kate Millett had just written her book, *Sexual Politics*. Germaine Greer had written *The Female Eunuch* and the topic of women's role in society was very much under discussion. Most of the

> "I was fortunate to have a father who believed that a daughter and a son must have equal rights. This was not usual in Pakistan when I was growing up."
>
> BENAZIR BHUTTO

girls at that time still thought that after leaving college they would get married, but a significant proportion thought they would like to work. I was very much encouraged by the entire Women's Movement. It was also the time when President Nixon was being impeached and I found it so empowering that the leader of the greatest superpower could be brought down by his own people. I came from a dictatorship, and I thought, I must go back and do what I could to empower my own people. It was a very good experience.

Swanee Hunt

My father was a tough, independent oilman, what they called a "wildcatter" in the days when you first had to find where the oil wells were. I think I inherited his bold "let's try this" kind of attitude. We weren't brought up in an élite kind of environment – we lived in a mansion, but it was still a very simple way of life, interestingly enough. My father drove himself to work and took his lunch in a brown paper bag.

He was said then to be the richest man in the country, some people said in the world, because that was before the Middle East oil bonanza. Another big influence in my early life was the Southern Baptist Church, which always gave me the comforting sense of being a child of God. Then I went to an excellent girls' school, which made me very much appreciate female power and strength.

Judi Dench

I was brought up in a theatre-loving family, and it must have been going to the theatre that influenced the way my life went. But I didn't want to be an actress at first. I just wanted to be a theatre designer – sets and costumes. That was what I set my heart on. I love drawing and my father was a very good painter, my whole family has painted.

Helen Prejean

My growing up was in a deeply Catholic family, very open to having someone in the family who devoted their life to religion. The nuns who taught me at school were energetic, alive, warm, intellectual women. I joined that community at a very young age, 18, but I knew what I wanted. I'd never been sure that I wanted to marry and have just one little family. There was part of me that wanted to be an educator, but I also wanted something broader. So I became a Sister, taught in a middle high school, 7th and 8th grade, and became Director of Religious Education at the Parish. Then in the mid 1960s, the Second Vatican Council called on us not to remove ourselves from the world but to plunge into the world, and its suffering people and its joys. The idea that within the context of the community we could help to transform the world is what led me to become one of the Sisters of St Joseph, and later to move into an African-American inner city housing project in 1980. It's while I was there, seeing what it was like to be poor and black and uneducated with the police beating you, and a minimum-pay job and no healthcare, that I understood how privileged I'd been as a young white woman growing up in Baton Rouge, Louisiana, in the '40s and '50s. So I immersed myself in the people to get to learn from them, and it was there that I was asked in 1982 to write to a person on Death Row.

Jody Williams

I believe that everything one experiences influences you in one way or another. My oldest brother was born deaf and developed schizophrenia in adolescence and we lived in a very small town in Vermont. My brother was different enough that kids were mean to him. I grew up defending him and it translated slowly into defending other people who, by no fault of their own, were the way they were.

> “My brother was different enough that kids were mean to him. I grew up defending him and it translated slowly into defending other people ...”
>
> JODY WILLIAMS

Kim Phuc

I was very influenced by my family, and by the love that they showed me. They took so much care of me when I was burned by the napalm, and it was a big sacrifice for them, especially my mum. I was in the hospital for 14 months. I was really disabled, and suffered so much with the pain that I cried a lot. But I thank God I didn't take anything for granted. I saw how my parents, my brother and sister, and all the people round us helped me, and so I tried my best. I went back to school but I'd lost one year of my grade 4. I really wanted to study, and so with that determination I jumped to grade 5.

We had lost everything in the war and had nowhere to live. My family only just survived. My left hand was so damaged that I couldn't move my fingers, and my skin was really deformed. So they just helped me to do constant exercises. My friends, my brother, my sister, my cousin, my mum and my dad, they were all so busy, but when they were at home they spent time with me. Their love and sacrifice really

> "My teens were the hardest because of the scars on my body. I thought I'd never get a boyfriend. That nobody would love me."
>
> KIM PHUC

helped me to move on. My teens were the hardest because of the scars on my body. I thought I'd never get a boyfriend. That nobody would love me. And I'd never get married and never have a baby.

Mairead Maguirev

I was born in Belfast in 1944. I grew up in a Catholic family of eight children, and was blessed to have just wonderful parents. My parents were a great influence on me, and they always believed in seeing the good in people, and working where you could to help them. I had travelled to Thailand and Russia before we started the Peace People movement in Northern Ireland in 1976, and I felt the movement was, in a sense, the continuation of a spiritual journey to a wider world. Then winning the Nobel Peace Prize helped me to be able to cope with what was a very difficult and challenging situation in Northern Ireland.

Louise Ridley

I always loved telling stories and writing, though I'm not sure where that came from. My mum and dad had very different careers from mine – my mum works in mental health and my dad was a banker. But my mum is a great communicator and my dad read lots of books like the entire Narnia, His Dark Materials and The Lord of the Rings series to me when I was young. I did win a poetry competition at school aged about ten, and was terribly proud of myself ... I also did some early work experience in journalism aged about 16, and got to spend a few days at ITN and in the press gallery of the House of Commons. It happened to be a busy news week: Alistair Campbell resigned so I spent an afternoon with some camera people chasing him around Westminster, and Dennis Thatcher passed away so I got to meet John Major when he was giving a tribute to him. From this I was convinced that journalism must be an incredibly exciting, busy and important job.

In another way my upbringing absolutely influenced my career path – I'm white, middle class and went to a great private school in London, which gave me a good education, contacts and confidence, which in turn helped me get into journalism, which is still sadly a business that's not very diverse or easy to access without money. Often a route into it is through who you know, or through the ability to do unpaid work experience in London, and recognizing that was an important moment for me. I try to acknowledge that my background helped me to get ahead and make a point of saying yes to everyone I can who asks for a coffee, advice or help.

Shami Chakrabarti

I'm sure that my upbringing must have affected my direction in life. My parents were the kind of people who always discussed difficult issues around the dining table. So from a very early age I was aware of the pressures, the natural tensions between the individual and the state. I think that I did grow up to challenge the consensus and to discuss quite difficult issues and not always to rush to judgment. When I was 12 years old and the news bulletins were full of chilling stories about the Yorkshire Ripper, that multiple rapist and murderer, I remember telling my father that this man was an animal, and speculating on what should be done to him when he was caught. My father said he didn't know how I could possibly support the death penalty. He asked me to imagine what it would be like to be the one innocent person in a million who had been convicted of murder, to know that nobody believed you, and to know that you were about to die. That conversation had a profound effect on me. I don't think that it's robbed me of any concern for victims of crime, but it put me in passionate opposition to the death penalty and gave me a concern about the rights of all defendants.

Nataša Kandić

I have a picture in my mind from when I was very young of watching children fighting on my street, and of hearing parents accusing other children of something their own children had done. I felt at the time that this was unfair and that I should tell the truth, say who was guilty, and never accuse others. So even when I was a child I always felt that it was important to fight for justice even in small ways.

Mary McAleese

I think our backgrounds are almost inescapable. My grandmother used to quote a phrase from an old proverb book, "What's learned in childhood is engraved on the stone," and there is a lot of truth in that. I grew up as one of nine children in Ardoyne, Belfast, in a poor parish, though *we* were not poor. My father and mother were frugal homemakers, hard on themselves but very good to their children and in a sense very self-sacrificing. Very typical of Irish parents of their generation. My mother and her brothers and sisters had 60 children between them, all of us living very close together. I grew up accustomed to having a lot of people and a lot of different personality types around me, so that was a good education. But in Ardoyne I was also very conscious that I was living in a virtually exclusively Protestant area. Though most of my friends were Protestant, I went to a Catholic school. So I grew up in that very complex Northern Ireland context of inter-faith with strong sectarian overtones.

I think that context led to the path that I am now on as President of Ireland. I am committed to bridge-building because I grew up in a world where the failure to build those bridges led to the loss of human life, and led to conflict in what has been a very macho world. A world where *women* were to be seen and not heard, never mind children. We wasted a lot of that life. Northern Ireland has at last turned a corner, and we now have people in government who never would have talked to each other in the past. It's interesting to have so many people say to me: "I wish I was 30 years younger." That tells me how many of us feel that our lives were robbed of peace of heart and mind by conflicts that we inherited, didn't create, and took a long time to resolve.

Carla Del Ponte

I had thought I would study medicine at university. But my father said, "You'll spend eight years of your life studying and afterwards you'll get married and never work, and so I'd just be spending money on you for nothing." So I chose law because that was only four years at university. From the beginning I wanted to do criminal law, to obtain justice for victims. Then, in 1980, I became an examining magistrate in Lugarno where I learned a lot about how to conduct criminal investigations while working against the Mafia and their money laundering through Swiss bank accounts. This kind of experience was extremely important in my work as Chief War Crimes Prosecutor at the United Nations. In the fight against organized crime you learn how to conduct an investigation, to stay focused and not to enlarge your investigations beyond the point where you have sufficient evidence for an indictment.

Yoko Ono

I rebelled against my upbringing. So it definitely influenced me.

Tanni Grey-Thompson

I was hugely influenced by the way my parents brought me up. Not specifically to go into sport, but to be questioning, have a strong mind, and believe in myself. I was certainly encouraged to do sport from quite a young age, partly I think to calm me down and to stop me being quite so irritating. I had so much energy. My parents always said, "You can mess around and do sport once you've got your qualifications," so I suppose their encouragement to finish my education with a degree did ultimately contribute towards my success as a wheelchair athlete.

Christiane Amanpour

At a very formative age I experienced revolution in my country, Iran. This turned my whole world upside down. It focused me and made me realize that I wanted to be a journalist.

Isabel Allende

I was brought up to be somebody's wife and a mother. Women of my generation in Chile seldom had superior education, so I was not really prepared to be a writer. However, I travelled extensively and I was a voracious reader. Also, my mother and my grandfather were good storytellers – I grew up listening to stories.

Kate Clinton

My early Catholic upbringing probably gave me a small gene of justice and of wanting to see more empowerment of women. I was a middle child with two older brothers, a younger brother and younger sister, and I learned early on that humour was the way that I could sort of neutralize my brothers. I mean they were all big football players and fairly overwhelming. I would make them laugh – it was a way to weaken them and to protect myself. So from those early days I learned the power of humour, and how very often it's the way to loosen people up.

> “I was brought up to be somebody’s wife and a mother.”
>
> ISABEL ALLENDE

Emma Bonino

Back home, when I was growing up, the person who had the most influence over me was my mother. She was a very independent person, commanding yet understanding, principled but also with an open-minded view of the world. But the single experience that influenced the direction I eventually took came later when I was in my mid-twenties. After going through an eye-opening personal experience, I started volunteer work in Milan with clandestine abortion clinics that helped ordinary women who were unable to pay for a private operation or to go abroad to have an abortion – at that time illegal in Italy. Applying the principles of civil disobedience, I then turned myself over to the police and was arrested. At the time, the campaign for a law to legalize abortion was a priority of the Italian Radical Party, so I soon joined it, becoming a Member of Parliament the following year. It was in 1976 and I was 27 years old.

> "If you face the world with enough confidence to know who you are and what your standards are, you may have setbacks but you don't doubt yourself or your decisions."
>
> MARIE COLVIN

Marie Colvin

Both my mother and my father made it clear that you could do whatever you set your mind to. I never felt that I had the traditional role of a female, so their most important influence on me was probably that they gave me confidence. If you face the world with enough confidence to know who you are and what your standards are, you may have setbacks but you don't doubt yourself or your decisions. I didn't start out as a journalist, I wanted to be a marine biologist.

Shirin Ebadi

When I was very young I was infatuated with this notion that later I found out to be justice. Injustice really bothered me. For example, if I saw a fight between two youngsters on the street, without knowing what the issue was, I usually supported the smaller one, and was often hit for intervening without a cause. My interest in justice is what led to my going to Law School. Also, my father was an attorney and I was used to discussions about legal issues at home. I trained to become a judge after I graduated from Law School because I believed that this could help me to bring about justice. After the Iranian revolution of 1979 I was told that as a woman I could not continue to be a judge. So I decided to work as an attorney, and in my law practice I picked the field of human rights because I thought that this way I could still help to bring justice to the world and my family. Sometimes I think that if my father had been a doctor, maybe I would have ended up being a doctor as well and I would have worked on AIDS issues. The feeling that I had for justice would have made me an activist anyway, even if I were a doctor. I think each person is born with certain characteristics and, of course, when they are nurtured they become the characteristics that will be carried into your life. I was raised in a well-educated family, modern and at the same time religious, and this background gave me the certain mentality that I have.

> "The feeling that I had for justice would have made me an activist anyway, even if I were a doctor."
>
> SHIRIN EBADI

Martha Lane Fox

I was never pushed in any particular direction. So I had the luxury of being allowed to think that I could become anything from a world-class actress to a prison governor or a prime minister. When I said I was going to start my own dot-com business, my parents would have been more surprised if I'd told them I wanted to go and work in a bank. The freedom they gave me to make my own way in life was probably the biggest influence on me.

Dagmar Havlová

I was brought up in a theatrical and artistic environment, which directed my life journey towards the arts and also led me to become independent, because my parents were often not at home in the evenings. From the age of 12 I was in charge of the whole household on the evenings when my parents were at work, and I took care of my older sister who was ill. I suppose the ability to make independent decisions has helped shape my life and also influenced my interest in social work mainly with the VIZE 97 Foundation that Václav and I started.

Sinéad O'Connor

As an Irish girl born into a theocracy, which Ireland was at the time, I was obviously influenced by Catholicism and by the country I grew up in. But I was principally influenced by

> “I was principally influenced by having to live in a situation of being severely abused by my mother. I suppose I couldn’t separate what was happening in the home from what was happening in the country.”
>
> SINÉAD O’CONNOR

having to live in a situation of being severely abused by my mother. I suppose I couldn’t separate what was happening in the home from what was happening in the country.

Mary Robinson

I was fortunate enough to have parents, both doctors, who encouraged me to believe that I had the same prospects as my four brothers of developing my full potential. My grandfather was a lawyer committed to law being about justice, and he very much influenced me, as I studied law, to see it as an instrument of social justice. When I went to Harvard Law School, it was at a time when there was a lot of questioning about the Vietnam War, about civil rights in the South, and even about the law itself and how it was being taught. It was very empowering.

Ann Leslie

My childhood background probably prepared me to be a foreign correspondent. My father was in an oil company and my family was very peripatetic, they lived all over the subcontinent, and I was first sent to boarding school in India at the age of four. When I went back to whichever city in India they were living in, it wouldn't be the same home that I had left. So, for example, I never really had any toys because there was no point in carting them all over the place. To a degree I got used to being peripatetic, and I was endlessly curious. Later, I was sent to boarding schools in England and didn't see my family more than once or twice a year. It forced me to become quite tough, even cold-blooded, self-sufficient and unsentimental about hearth and home.

Paula Rego

I couldn't say early experiences influenced the direction of my life, because when you're young you have no control over anything, so it is more what your parents are like and what they want you to do that counts. I was very lucky. I lived in Portugal and my father was a very liberal person considering that we lived under a dictatorship. He wanted me to leave, because Portugal was not a country for a woman. Mind you, it wasn't a country for men either, because it was such a fascist place. I did go away at 16.

Soledad O'Brien

My parents influenced what I value in life, absolutely. What they value is kindness, goodness, respect. I remember early on when people would ask me, "Oh, your parents must be so proud that you are on television." The reality is that they could not care less. I think they are glad I have a job and that I seem happy. In a way my dad had an influence on me, because he loved the news and so I used to watch the news all the time as a child – serious news. I'm sure that played a big role in why I went to CNN.

Hanan Ashrawi

My parents brought me up to value myself and at the same time to recognize that one's rights are not exclusive but depend on other people's rights. They also taught me to stand up for what is right, and not be intimidated or limited. To explore and to go beyond the given and accepted. My father, in particular, taught us that women were equal to men and made sure that we did not accept any discrimination. That's the way my parents treated us at home. Education, reading and openness to different ideas and different worlds were instilled in us at a very early age. All these things did give me an advantage, I would say, a sense of identity, self-confidence and self-reliance. At the same time, a sense of humanism, accepting others.

Mary Kayitesi Blewitt

As a child born after my family had fled from Rwanda in 1959, my refugee upbringing and experiences must have played a big part in what I do now to help the survivors of the 1994 Rwanda genocide. As a refugee, you didn't feel that you were like the people around you – the shadow of something just behind you always told you that you were not like everyone else. It made my family and me feel very apart from other people and events. When the 1994 genocide happened, I didn't feel I had the right to blame anyone. Without the previous experiences in my life, I would probably have found it very difficult to move on.

Kathy Kelly

I was very much influenced by my teachers, most of whom were nuns. Service to others and sharing their resources was a way of life. A contrary influence was the sense of fear that I felt in my own neighbourhood, a fear of mixing with people who were different. There was also, to some extent, a sense of fatalism, that you couldn't really change the way things were, and if you tried to do that, you might be acting too big for your breeches. So I'm very grateful to my parents for their love and care and for providing the sense of security that helps young people eventually find their way.

> “I resisted the artistic route as long as I could, but it was just my path.”
>
> PALOMA PICASSO

Paloma Picasso

I resisted the artistic route as long as I could, but it was just my path. My mother, Françoise Gilot, tried not to overdo that side of bringing us up. She knew we already saw our father working all day, so she used to lock her studio when she herself was painting. I remember quite often going onto the balcony to look in at her, but I think she was right to protect her own artistic life. She took us to museums and so forth but she didn't overdo it, so that we'd still think of it as a treat. To an extent, I have overcome my fear of having such a big name to live up to. But I don't draw for the sake of drawing. I only draw when I have a design idea for a watch or a piece of jewellery, because designing is my life.

Bianca Jagger

I don't think there is a single person who was not influenced by their upbringing. When people ask me why I decided to embark on a life defending human rights, I always respond that I was brought up in Nicaragua in a dictatorship. And I shall never forget the impact my parent's divorce had on my existence. Overnight my well-to-do, privileged life was turned upside down. Once my mother was divorced and became a working woman, she was treated as a second-rate citizen because of her gender. Through this, I first understood the meaning of discrimination.

Tracey Emin

My parents, who were not married, never expected anything of me. Mum was poor, and Dad left us. I stopped going to school when I was about 13. I think my lack of education and the amount of mental freedom that I had helped my art. I had no restrictions. I could do whatever I wanted. I've always been creative and I'm good at creating space that didn't exist before – going beyond art. It's like there's a place in the world with nothing in it, and I'm trying to make things for it. My mum always says that if I hadn't done art, I probably wouldn't have seen the point of being here. I wouldn't have felt weighted.

Marion Cotillard

All my early experiences have influenced the direction I've taken in life. I changed direction at a certain point because I felt I was moving away from who I am. I learn every day and try to stay close to myself. Being aware that you're headed in the wrong direction, and understanding why, so you can find the power to change, is a great experience.

> “My lack of education and the amount of mental freedom that I had helped my art. I had no restrictions. I could do whatever I wanted.”
>
> TRACEY EMIN

Mariane Pearl

My mother deeply influenced my direction in life by allowing me to choose my own path. She gave me the confidence to believe in free will. I think that regardless of where we come from, we potentially have the ability to create a new person – if not entirely, at least in our foundations or beliefs.

Severn Cullis-Suzuki

We're definitely products of our childhood. As a spokesperson for the environment I had great role models in my dad, who is well known in Canada, my mum, and my grandparents, who took my sister and me camping and fishing and out into nature ever since we could walk. We grew up fishing right in the heart of Vancouver, which we still do in the summertime when the smelts come in to spawn. I think it's very important for city people not to become totally disconnected from nature and the living sources of what they eat. Reconnection is essential in the city, and I was lucky to have that growing up.

WHAT INSPIRES YOU IN LIFE? | 2

Mary McAleese

The big inspiration in my life is, and always has been, that great commandment, "Love one another," and the outworking of that. As soon as I heard that message, it made a lot of sense. It seemed to me to be the kind of thing that could wriggle its way through all sorts of intractable places and spaces and could forge much more hope-filled connections from one human being to another. It also explained the world in context to me, and explained death. But in particular, it explained to me how we could resolve conflict in life. I'm talking about a discipline of love that really has to do with forgiveness. Not necessarily forgetfulness, but forgiveness and an ability to find the decent and the human in others. Try to find the common ground, and if you cannot find common ground, find compassion. Those are the things that inspire me most in life.

Isabel Allende

Other people's lives, the books I read and the places I go inspire me. Most of my books come from a deep sense of memory. I write because I want to remember.

Kathy Kelly

People who stand up for disadvantaged people inspire me. I'm also very inspired when people don't let inconvenience get in the way of living according to their values. Karl Meyer inspired me in my late twenties when he went to prison for

> “Most of my books come from a deep sense of memory. I write because I want to remember.”
>
> ISABEL ALLENDE

refusing to pay taxes while trillions of dollars were being put into weapon systems. I'm inspired by Mairead Maguire because she is fearless in her readiness to champion various human rights causes, and never swerves from saying things even when they might place her at risk. I'm also very inspired by people who choose to live more simply and in a more sustainable way. I see this in the younger generation, biking right through snow, ice and storms just because they refuse to succumb to the pressures of car culture.

Helen Prejean

Now that I have become engaged with people on Death Row, and with murder victims' families, and with the struggles of poor people, it is the worth of each human being that inspires me. I met two women on Death Row in Pennsylvania and looked into their faces, and immediately my heart moved out to them, and I was lifted up because no matter what they have done, people are worth more than the worst act of their life. I'm fired and energized by the potential within the human person, by being with them, shouldering their burdens with them, struggling for their lives. It's like being lifted up on a huge wave of energy.

Bianca Jagger

I am inspired by the hope that one can make a difference and can have a meaningful life. Probably the most inspiring and rewarding experience I ever had was to evacuate a little boy of eight from Tuzla during the Bosnian War while the city was being besieged and shelled in 1995. He needed to have an operation for a hole in the heart. His name is Mohammed and he is alive in Bosnia. I went to visit a children's ward and was asked to evacuate Mohammed and a beautiful girl called Sabina who had leukaemia. There was an incredible amount of red tape in order to take them out of there, including the need to find a hospital that was prepared to give them free treatment. For eight weeks I did everything to overcome the obstacles before I was finally able to cross into Croatia with them in a four-wheel-drive along a really dangerous road. Sabina died while we were waiting for visas and a flight to America. I appealed for help for Mohammed on CBS, and Columbia Presbyterian Hospital made a commitment to carry out the operation that saved him when we reached New York. The experience taught me that it is incredibly difficult and risky to take children out of a country at war. The important thing is to bring doctors and medical supplies in.

Emma Bonino

What has always inspired me is the fact that the status quo can be modified. In other words, that the world can be changed for the better.

Maya Angelou

Well my brother Bailey inspired me. He was two years older than me and very short, but he was smart. When I was eight, I was sexually abused by my mother's boyfriend. He was killed three days after he was tried for raping me, and I thought he had died because I'd said something wrong at the trial. For a long time after that I stopped talking to anyone except Bailey. He would speak softly to me, and tell me I was smart. So I just figured I could learn anything, and I tried.

Swanee Hunt

I'm inspired by suffering and the need to help. My mother said I was always like that. I'd see a bedraggled kitten and bring it home. So I guess I've been bringing little kittens home for a long time.

Kate Clinton

I absolutely love to laugh and this inspires me to go on and on. Sometimes when I am performing and have kept an audience in hysterics for, like, 90 minutes, I think that I'd love to be in the audience myself. I love to be able to do that

> "What brings joy and inspiration to a life is its purpose."
>
> MARIANE PEARL

to people so that when they come out of a show, they say, "You know, my face hurts, I pulled muscles in my stomach!" So laughter really does inspire me. I mean, you learn to put yourself on the line doing comedy, and I think that it's good practice for the political work that we do. I just think there is massive national Attention Deficit Disorder in America. Hardly anybody pays attention, everybody is multi-tasking so madly that they're not really present, and real laughter is a good antidote for that.

Mariane Pearl

I am inspired by life itself, and by great ideals like justice, and by the ability those ideals have to trigger greatness in us. What brings joy and inspiration to a life is its purpose. I can't live without the inspiration I draw from other human beings. People who stand up alone inspire me, like Nelson Mandela. Humanism as a science fascinates me, and it is inspiring to think that individuals might very well be the agents for any reliable change in our world. Faith and love are my main sources of inspiration.

Mary Robinson

I was inspired by my father as a medical practitioner, because he was very committed to patients having access to medicines and to healthcare, whether they could pay or not. He also related very much to individuals and their right to be treated with dignity even if they were old or inarticulate, and he had great patience and a great listening quality. That really inspired me to an early understanding that we are all equal in dignity and worth.

Ann Leslie

I'm inspired by curiosity, really, learning about the cultures and travails of other countries and meeting their people, many of them deeply traumatized by war, famine and oppression. I'm often inspired by their unbelievable stoicism. I'm certainly not inspired by the idea that, as a journalist, I am doing a huge amount of good in the world. It's important to get the story out, but I think too many journalists like to think that they are far more influential and important than they really are.

Tracey Emin

I'm my own driving force, but as I get older, it becomes more and more difficult. I find nature is something really incredibly beautiful and I would like to be able to connect with it more, but it feels so far away from me. I admit that emotional gut feelings drive me too, twist something in me. If I was to fall madly in love, the twist on that could push a whole load of new work, could inspire something. Or it could send me to bed for days and days. So, though I hate to say it, it's definitely myself that inspires me.

Severn Cullis-Suzuki

I grew up loving nature, and I find that it's incredibly rejuvenating. That quiet, that peace that you have when you are standing beside a stream or out on the ocean or in a forest is essential.

Benazir Bhutto

When I went back to Pakistan and my father was imprisoned and unjustly executed under military rule, my motivation was really anger at the injustice. And when people turned towards me to lead them, I did. By becoming the first elected woman Prime Minister of a Muslim country, I broke the barrier of tradition and inspired many other Muslim women. I remember, when I started my career and I used to go on election tours, that there would be little boys who would come to my meetings, but never little girls, and after I became Prime Minister I was so very happy to see that men brought their daughters with them. It had become acceptable and respectable for girls to be seen in society. I met an African woman once who told me that she was managing a utility, and when she got pregnant her boss said she had to leave the job, and she said, "Why, Benazir Bhutto can have a baby and run a country, so why can't I run a utility and have a child too?" And he accepted her argument!

Joan Baez

I find courage inspiring, and also nature.

Jung Chang

I owe my inspiration for my first book to my grandmother and mother. In 1988, my mother came to London to stay with me and for the first time, away from the political and social confines of China, she was able to talk freely and frankly. Once she started, she couldn't stop. During the six months she stayed with me, she talked every day, leaving me 60 hours of tape recordings. Those tapes were the basis of *Wild Swans*.

Soledad O'Brien

What inspires me outside of work is love for my family, embracing the stress, and the craziness, and the chaos of living with four small children. And in my career, I'm definitely inspired by the challenge of telling a good, fair story. I mean it's really exciting to be in a breaking story, and to run around and have as your job and your responsibility the weight of getting it right. You have got to get it right.

Carla Del Ponte

In my professional life what inspires me is justice. This is what motivates me to do my best day by day, to develop my ability to achieve compensation for victims, and to see that real justice is done. What has been extremely important for me in my entire professional career is honesty and truth. I could never be a politician, for example, because mediation and compromise are not my way of doing things. Because my career was based on being a prosecutor, compromise has never been an option for me.

Tanni Grey-Thompson

I'm probably inspired by my own self-criticism. I never think I've done enough, so I keep on striving to be the best I possibly can.

Louise Ridley

I love it when I see someone really acting out their principles. In the words of the rapper Perico Princess (a quote shared with me by the very inspiring BBC journalist Megha Mohan): "resources not compliments" is a great mantra. It's so easy to share positive words or sentiments, but it's a lot more helpful to actively give someone access to your knowledge, contacts or experience.

> “In my professional life what inspires me is justice. This is what motivates me to do my best day by day, to develop my ability to achieve compensation for victims, and to see that real justice is done.”
>
> CARLA DEL PONTE

Yoko Ono

I'm inspired by adversity.

Martha Lane Fox

I'm inspired by seeing other people's excitement in things, to see them really charged up by something – to right a wrong or support an issue. In my business life, I don't think I could be involved in something where I didn't feel that kind of buzz and energy and real passion for the product. You know, I really loved the concept of lastminute.com. I love the feeling my karaoke business gives the customers.

Dagmar Havlová

I am inspired by the arts, certainly. Also by nature and by contact with clever and educated people.

Marie Colvin

The more I work in journalism, the more I care passionately about exposing injustice to the world and writing about it. For example, you go back to the Vietnam War, which essentially ended because, over an extremely long period, journalism on the ground exposed what was happening and people in America started saying, "Not in our name." In Iraq, I think the best thing was to remove Saddam Hussein who was a murderous dictator. So many mistakes have been made since then. Maybe policy hasn't changed, but if you weren't hearing what has been going on in Iraq, how could there even be a debate? I'm inspired by just being able to get something across and make some kind of difference with my writing.

Mary Kayitesi Blewitt

The genocide in Rwanda that took 50 members of my own family has inspired me to do something about building instead of destroying. If something horrible happens to you, the only way you can get around it is to look deeper to see what you can do to make it better. Genocide is very difficult to explain to anyone, and when you can't explain things to people, you can't expect them to be able to understand. If I can't find the words for it, I'm inspired to try to show the pain and grief of it in a different way.

Christiane Amanpour

Courage in all its forms inspires me, whether moral or physical. Also, beauty in all its forms.

Hanan Ashrawi

At a very subjective level I've always been inspired by my daughters, by the fact that I am a mother, and now a grandmother. So it's a very personal thing. The collective also comes into play. I've always been quite moved and impassioned by the rights of the Palestinian people. The Palestinians have suffered great injustices through no fault of their own. They really are victims of history and they continue to suffer, to live in pain, deprivation and hardship, without protection. This injustice sometimes makes me quite angry, but at the same time it also motivates me to try to do something about it. Not only to right the wrongs, but also to set the record straight: the Palestinian narrative and reality.

> "The genocide in Rwanda that took 50 members of my own family has inspired me to do something about building instead of destroying ... I'm inspired to try to show the pain and grief of it in a different way."
>
> MARY KAYITESI BLEWITT

Mairead Maguire

I am inspired by my faith and my prayer. I'm so very blessed in my wonderful family, my great husband, five children and five grandchildren. And other people inspire me – I just see great courage and resilience in them.

Judi Dench

I think what inspires me is seeing and sharing the enthusiasm of a group of people. That is the bit I like best about acting. I never wanted to do a one-woman show, for instance. I need the influence and the kind of spark off other people that you get when you are rehearsing and when it's working wonderfully. I love that.

Paula Rego

Art inspires me. I've always loved to draw.

Kim Phuc

It's love that really inspires me. My Christian faith, which I found in 1982, has changed my life completely.

“Other people inspire me – I just see great courage and resilience in them.”

MAIREAD MAGUIRE

> "Just being alive inspires me. Then my children are a big inspiration – they're always the thing that keeps you going and gives you life."
>
> SINÉAD O'CONNOR

Shami Chakrabarti

Ultimately, I'm just inspired by people, my family, my friends – very tangible, very real things like that. I have a young son who I find incredibly inspirational. I think that there is something special about human beings, and that most people in the world, if you actually boil down their experience and their concerns, do believe in the precious nature of human life and human rights values.

Sinéad O'Connor

Just being alive inspires me. Then my children are a big inspiration – they're always the thing that keeps you going and gives you life. So I guess the thing I most aspire to is being a good mother.

Jane Fonda

Friends and family inspire me. One of them is Eve Ensler, the author of *The Vagina Monologues*, who is a force of nature. I have a handful of friends who inspire me to be braver and stronger. Young girls in particular, teenage girls who haven't capitulated to the gender norms of our culture, who have struck out on their own and are becoming feisty activists – they inspire me. And I'm often inspired by books.

Wangari Maathai

When you think about what has inspired you in life, it's very difficult to point to just one thing, but my mother was probably very influential in the early part of my life and after that my teachers, especially the Irish and Italian sisters – they were very important to me.

WHAT MOST PROVOKES YOU TO ANGER, AND DO YOU BELIEVE IN FORGIVENESS? | 3

Swanee Hunt

I was most angry when I became an adult and the Dallas Petroleum Club forbade me from entering the dining room because I was a woman ... and when I was told by the men in my family that I didn't have a place in the boardroom of our company. That was personal anger, and I dealt with it by leaving home. I have developed a huge capacity for forgiveness, and that's partly because of the women with whom I work in Rwanda or Liberia. They've gone through real hell yet have found a way to reconcile with the actual perpetrators of the violence as these people are brought back into the community. So every time I start feeling I can't ever forgive someone for something, I remember what we're asking those women to do, and I say to myself that I will find a way. If they can find that sort of capacity to forgive, so can I.

Bianca Jagger

Probably if I were to close my eyes and think of a few who have angered me the most, it would include George Bush and Tony Blair. What angers me is the impunity with which George Bush has acted, tearing up the international rule of law, institutionalizing the use of torture, completely disregarding the need to sign up to the Kyoto Protocol. To think we are not doing anything about Darfur. To think that the United States is still permitted to have Guantánamo Bay. There is an endless list of things. Do I believe in forgiveness? Yes, I do.

> “Hypocrisy is at the top of the list of things that make me angry.”
>
> EMMA BONINO

Emma Bonino

Hypocrisy is at the top of the list of things that make me angry. And to forgive hypocritical behaviour is usually rather counter-productive.

Jane Fonda

I live by forgiveness. I think we are all walking wounded to one degree or another, and the only way we can begin to heal is first to understand the nature of the wound and then to forgive. Then healing begins. You can't forgive until you have understood the wound. Otherwise it's like sewing up a bullet hole with the bullet still inside. I don't feel anger when a veteran of Vietnam hates me and says something cruel. I feel sadness. I feel fury at men like Donald Rumsfeld and Henry Kissinger. It's not they should have known better – they did know better – but cynicism rules their lives, and lives are lost as a result. I remember watching two documentaries side by side – *The Fog of War* about Robert McNamara, and *The Trials of Henry Kissinger.* I felt fury watching Kissinger and none at all when I watched McNamara, because there I

> "I live by forgiveness. I think we are all walking wounded to one degree or another, and the only way we can begin to heal is first to understand the nature of the wound and then to forgive. Then healing begins."
>
> JANE FONDA

saw a man who has suffered deeply because of his mistakes as Defense Secretary. He has apologized for them. Kissinger never will.

Maya Angelou

I believe in anger. Anger's like fire, it can burn out all the dross and leave some positive things. But what I don't believe in is bitterness. Forgiveness is imperative because you don't want to carry that weight around, who needs to? And it will throw you down. It doesn't help you to live life. I don't make myself vulnerable if I can help it.

Yoko Ono

Injustice makes me angry. Forgiving is releasing in order to walk away. Yes, I believe in releasing.

Kate Clinton

Anger is a sin for Catholics. In my family, if you got angry you were sent to your room. It's quite different with my Indian-born girlfriend who comes from a very chatty and explosive family, so she's been wonderful for me. I've now learned that you can get angry, and let it out, and feel so much better. In terms of forgiveness, I think I am more forgiving if someone shows a willingness to change their behaviour.

Ann Leslie

Anger isn't useful because you tend to lose your temper and that puts you at a disadvantage. Of course, I get angry as a journalist – with drunken checkpoint thugs, stupid bureaucrats, obstructive men with guns – but you have to control the anger. Actually if you can channel what you're feeling inside into a cold strategic plan, then it's useful, but I never start screaming at anyone. Other people do, and sometimes it works. I cry quite a lot, though I try not to ever since I started wearing eye makeup, because it makes

> "I believe in anger. Anger's like fire, it can burn out all the dross and leave some positive things. But what I don't believe in is bitterness."
>
> MAYA ANGELOU

a terrible mess of your face. But strategic tears are quite useful, particularly in countries where you're playing the role of some silly woman who's terribly emotional.

I think you should forgive, not for the sake of the person you're forgiving but for your own sake. Being unable to forgive is hugely destructive to oneself. I say that, but I'm always amazed and awed by people who've been through the most horrendous experiences – like concentration camps or repeated rapes by soldiers in a war – who do forgive. I'm not sure I could.

Mariane Pearl

Injustice angers me at the most fundamental level. I feel that we need that anger. Or you might call it an indignation deep enough to give you the stamina to act. Sometimes forgiveness works, but in my case I have found it an insufficient response to the events I was confronting. If someone hurts you for real, more than forgiving that person you need to prove him or her wrong in what they are trying to accomplish by sending an equally powerful but opposing message. Forgiveness probably comes when you are mentally and spiritually way ahead of the person you need to forgive.

Sinéad O'Connor

I couldn't have grown up the way I did and not learn forgiveness. It's the main thing an abused child learns. I guess personally I get most angry when I feel I am being disrespected on the grounds that I'm a female, when someone deals with me in a different way to how they'd deal with a male. A plumber working on my house used to say things to me like, "Don't get in a tizzy!" when I challenged him about being messy, and I just wanted to smash his face in.

Mary Robinson

I do feel a sense of anger that is slow-burning, but very much there, about the unfairness of our world. For example, the unfairness that goes on in world trade, which is stacked on the side of the better-off countries and large corporations. I've tried to channel my anger into energy to seek change. I do believe in forgiveness. I have had a lot of experience with it in the context of Northern Ireland, observing the wonderful capacity to forgive of those who have suffered terrible pain and loss. And indeed, I've contributed to a book in honour of such a woman, Una O'Higgins O'Malley, that is all about forgiveness. She died, having been very much involved in peace and reconciliation in Ireland.

Benazir Bhutto

Well, I am a strong believer in forgiveness because I feel that inability to forgive makes one bitter, and I remember my father telling me this in my last meeting with him in his death cell. He said, "I don't want my hanging to make you bitter. You have to forgive and move on." I was very angry when my father was executed, but somehow that cycle came to a close when I was elected Prime Minister of Pakistan, because it seemed that justice had been done. I have seen so much suffering in my life because of economic circumstances or social circumstances or political persecution that I empathize with what the victims are going through, but I feel that one has to try and change things for the better rather than let that emotion develop into anger.

Nataša Kandić

I'm angry when I see that the victims of terrorism and war are always the poor people. Those who have money and position always find ways of escaping. In "ethnic cleansing" it's always the women and children who are the victims, who wait at home fearful of what will happen to them and of soldiers coming to kill them. I don't know about forgiveness. How can one forgive somebody who kills innocent people, makes thousands and thousands of people homeless and takes away their identities? To ask Muslims to forgive Serbs for what happened in Bosnia and Kosovo is, I think, the wrong

> “If we are stuck in the past I believe we destroy our creativity, we destroy our imagination to do things differently, and we destroy our own inner peace of mind.”
>
> MAIREAD MAGUIRE

approach, because we should never forget what happened in the past. We should try to remember without hate and try to show respect for others. I'm not sure that forgiveness is part of this process.

Mairead Maguire

I feel anger when I see real injustice and when I see unnecessary suffering perpetrated on people. I feel anger when I think of children dying of starvation. We live in a world of plenty, and if we really had the political will we could alleviate poverty. I feel anger when I think of all the money being wasted by governments on nuclear weapons and war, which kills many people and is a waste of our best scientific brains and a waste of precious human lives. But I tell myself that we have to convert our anger into positive action and demand that our governments solve these problems. I believe passionately in forgiveness. I believe it's the key to peace and that it should be unconditional.

We have seen a lot of wonderful acts of forgiveness here in Ireland. Just let me give you one example. Three of my sister Ann's children were killed in 1976 in the Troubles here in Northern Ireland. This happened in a clash between an active service unit of the IRA and the British Army. Ann herself was dangerously ill at the time. After she recovered, and learned to walk again, one of her first acts was a compassionate visit to the mother of the young IRA man who had been in the accident that killed her children. When I asked her why she did that, because the mother didn't even share the same politics as we did and her son had been an IRA gunman, she said, "She was a mother who'd also lost her son." You know I think that kind of compassion for others and forgiveness are very necessary if we're to change the world today. We can't live in the past. If we are stuck in the past I believe we destroy our creativity, we destroy our imagination to do things differently, and we destroy our own inner peace of mind.

Isabel Allende

I am angry at the abuse of power and the power to abuse. I am angry at the way women and children are treated in most of the world. And I am angry at fundamentalists and fanatics who try to impose their beliefs on others.

Yes, I believe in forgiveness but I think it is important not to forget, so that the same mistakes are not repeated. Forgiveness and reconciliation start with truth.

Christiane Amanpour

What provokes me to anger is wanton cruelty, injustice, racism and intolerance. I only believe in forgiveness in some instances. I think there are some crimes that are so great they can never be forgiven. On the other hand, I also believe in acceptance, understanding and moving on, but I think that sometimes you cannot forgive or forget some of the worst crimes and injustices.

Marie Colvin

Cruelty and people not acknowledging others as human beings like themselves makes me furious. I had to face seeing someone like Saddam Hussein in a courtroom, angry and impudent, and with no remorse when he had the blood of hundreds of thousands of people on his hands. What he did was inexcusable. Would I forgive him? No. I don't think he deserved forgiveness.

> “I think there are some crimes that are so great they can never be forgiven.”
>
> CHRISTIANE AMANPOUR

Mary McAleese

Bullying is really what angers me most. Any kind of bullying, whether it is at the level of little children bullying one another, right the way through to institutional bullying, or to national bullying by governments, or to the macro scale of imperialism and colonialism. Also socialism, communism, all those things that attempt to bully people into stereotypes, into boxes, to rob them of being who they are, what they are and what they want to be.

I don't find forgiveness particularly difficult. I mean it's a discipline that I observed in my own home. I'm very lucky in that I suffer from almost instant amnesia in relation to slights or hurts. I don't gather them up and collect them. I don't have a place inside me like there is in a computer, that limbo where, no matter what you delete, it's still there to be dragged up 20 years later. I'm very grateful for that, because I have met so many people in life who are so bogged down by bitterness that it continues to rob them of the joy of the present and joy of the future. I couldn't ever see myself living like that. It isn't that I haven't been hurt enough all the way through the Troubles. There were murder attempts on my family. I lost many good friends, and I mean decent, wonderful people, so there was plenty of opportunity for bitterness if you wanted to be bitter. People talk about closure, and I think I understand what they mean by that. I think it is actually very important for the generations to come to remember the cost of all this and the cost in human lives, so that they never drift easily back into conflict. I know with the distilled wisdom of hindsight that once that genie is out of the bottle, once you stop listening to each other, it's an animal out of control, absolutely out of control, and to try and get it back into the bottle again, well it took us 40 years here, and 4,000 people dead, and I don't know how many other people hurt and injured and disabled and emotionally disabled. So I think remembering is important.

Dagmar Havlová

I'm driven to anger by slovenliness and by my own negative characteristics, which I am working on, but which always rise to the surface when I least expect it. Anger is one of these negative characteristics, and an inability to control myself. Violence, xenophobia and disloyalty in people make me angry, and I especially hate it when somebody lies. The only time I ever slapped my daughter was when she lied to me. But I do believe in forgiveness.

Mary Kayitesi Blewitt

Lack of justice angers me, the feeling that terrible things have been done with impunity. Rwandans are told they should reconcile and forgive each other. But without justice, genocide could happen again. I can't forgive the atrocities in Rwanda and Darfur. I can't forgive the world for having stood by when my family was killed. There are so many to forgive. So many different levels of forgiveness. If my neighbour came to me and said, "I'm sorry, I killed your brother," we could sit around the table and talk about it. With time to think about it, absorb it, live with it, go through the healing process, eventually I'd find it in myself to forgive. But I don't know who killed my father, who killed my sister, or who killed my neighbour. I need to think about those people and deal with them one by one. As well as all this Christian forgiveness, we should focus on justice. No one is looking at the root causes of all these atrocities or thinking about finding and punishing the perpetrators. We must find a way of stopping these horrors.

Martha Lane Fox

I quickly get impatient about things, but not often really angry. People who make sweeping assumptions about things without really understanding often make me very irritable. Things that are clearly unfair or unjust also drive me to be quite quick-tempered. Also disparities in wealth or justice ... which all sounds very high-minded, but I don't think I'm too uncontrolled a person. I absolutely believe in forgiveness. I think it's bad and sad to harbour resentment and feelings of hatred against people. Admittedly, if I had a child who had been murdered or something hideous like that it would be very different, but I hope that I would always be able to find it in myself eventually to forgive.

Hanan Ashrawi

Injustice angers me, deliberate and wilful injustice, which is happening persistently in Palestine to a whole nation, a whole people. It's not just a political issue to me – it's a personal and human issue, an issue of values and morality. Of course I believe in forgiveness, but there has to be a condition – recognition of guilt. It seems to me that persistent cruelty can only be forgiven when it stops. Once people admit culpability and guilt, once they show a willingness to stop, then of course forgiveness has to follow.

Shami Chakrabarti

It's possibly after I've been angry that I'm in most need of forgiveness. What provokes me to anger? Obviously, I'm going to say injustice. Complacency, insensitivity, thoughtlessness, dishonesty, but perhaps complacency more than anything. People who think they're born to rule and don't feel, as perhaps they once did, the privilege and the awesome responsibility that comes with power. But I believe in forgiveness because we're all redeemable. I don't really believe we are all inherently good or evil. Good and evil things happen in the world, often caused by human beings, but I think we all have potential. Perhaps that's where my belief in human rights really comes from.

> "I cannot change what happened to me, but I can change what I do about it."
>
> KIM PHUC

Kim Phuc

Everything used to make me angry because I always asked myself, "Why me?" Why did they start the war and make me suffer? I tried to smile and move on, to be really positive, but deep, deep, deep inside my heart, I was living with hatred. I hated everyone because I was not normal. I knew that forgiveness was good for me, but I could not do it at the time ... not until 1982 when I became a Christian. Then I asked God to help me as I couldn't do it alone. How could I love my enemies? How could I forgive them? My heart was like a cup of bitter coffee, which I had to pour out every day – my own darkness, my hatred and bitterness, my sorrow, my anger. I learned to pour a little out every day until my cup was empty. Then God filled my cup with love, with forgiveness, and that's the moment when I felt that my heart completely healed. I cannot change what happened to me, but I can change what I do about it. I'm learning to forgive all the people who caused my suffering. I don't know their names. I just say: "I pray for the pilot, I pray for the man who ordered the bombing." I've moved on.

Carla Del Ponte

I'm most angered by people who lie. Yes, I believe in forgiveness, but justice must come first and then forgiveness, in the right sequence. For example, it's difficult now to expect victims of armed conflicts in the Balkans or in Africa to pardon their oppressors while we are still in the process of seeking justice for them. It's too early to just start again and say let's forget what happened. Reconciliation is important but justice comes first.

Jung Chang

While I was writing the biography of Mao I was constantly angry or outraged at what he did to our people. He was responsible for 70 million deaths and yet today his portrait is still displayed in Tiananmen Square, and his corpse is still lying in state for people to worship. I do believe in forgiveness, but here we are talking about evil on a gigantic scale. Last year when I was back in China, I went to my father's and grandmother's tombs with my mother. She is usually very

> "Mao never shed a tear for all those who were executed or persecuted to suicide under his rule. He was utterly pitiless to his people. I don't feel I can ever forgive him."
>
> JUNG CHANG

calm and optimistic, but she began to weep uncontrollably, and then I thought of all the tens of millions of other victims and their families. Towards the end of Mao's life his overriding emotion was self-pity, he was constantly in tears because he felt he hadn't made it. But he never shed a tear for all those who were executed or persecuted to suicide under his rule. He was utterly pitiless to his people. I don't feel I can ever forgive him.

Joan Baez

The stupidity of pig-headed people who are intelligent enough not to be that way makes me angry. But I embrace forgiveness wholeheartedly. I don't think we can be whole without it.

Shirin Ebadi

What makes me most angry is talking to people who have closed their eyes to reality, to the reality of life, and are prejudiced in their opinions. When I come into contact with these kinds of people I become angry, but what I have learned is that talking to these people is of no use, so when I encounter them I just have to leave. But I certainly believe in forgiveness, and this is why I am against capital punishment.

> “I embrace forgiveness wholeheartedly. I don’t think we can be whole without it.”
>
> JOAN BAEZ

Tracey Emin

About 12 years ago I become particularly angry about HIV and AIDS. I think a lot of people in Western society feel that the AIDS pandemic in Africa is so far away. I’m really angry that there isn’t something done about it. I can donate a piece of work to a charity that will sell for £200,000, but the AIDS charities that I’m involved with, like the Elton John AIDS Foundation and the Terrence Higgins Trust, will use that money to help directly. It seems to take so long for other AIDS programmes to make a difference.

I don’t know if I could forgive someone if they killed my child. I personally have been able to turn things around in terms of forgiving people who have done things to me. I was raped and sexually abused as a child but I forgive the people who did it, because if I didn’t, I wouldn’t be able to carry on. I’ve had the ability to do that through my work, by using those events in my life and working them through. But it’s very, very difficult to forget things. It’s a corny cliché, to forgive but not forget, but it’s very true.

Paula Rego

The way women are treated, the unfairness of certain regimes and how they treat women, makes me very angry. I saw it all happen in Portugal when I was young, and it took so many years to see any kind of equality, if you could call it that. Even now, it's doubtful. I believe in forgiveness, but I think that you can only forgive if it's something that's actually happened to you. You can't forgive if it's something that has happened to somebody else.

Soledad O'Brien

I don't like being lied to in an interview. But I am really very slow to anger. I have the kind of job where you see a lot of very tough things and you live through other people's lives and you see some of the tough times they have had. It's hard not to feel like an idiot for being angry about something minor like a broken dryer. I do believe in forgiveness. It's really clearing off your own plate as opposed to carrying around baggage in your head for a long time, so in a way it's almost a selfish thing to do. I'm happy to forgive people and move on.

Wangari Maathai

Selfishness and unwillingness to give others a chance is something I find very annoying. I definitely believe in forgiveness, we all have to learn to forgive. We all make mistakes, and you can't make peace if you can't forgive.

Kathy Kelly

I don't think anger is a bad element in peacemaking, but it's best to try to channel our anger about war or injustice or cruelty towards trying to create a very different set of circumstances. I spent a year in prison once, and concluded that women in prison didn't threaten society nearly as much as people who were building nuclear weapons and weapons of mass destruction, people who were depleting the ozone layer even further, people who were contributing to our environmental disasters by continuing an addictive consumption of the world's fossil fuels. These are the things that ought to terrify us, that really are the greatest threats to survival and decent livelihoods for people in the future. But I think that we won't solve those problems through an angry reaction but by channelling our anger into creative, productive and thoughtful approaches. Sometimes we should slow down, take a deep breath and feel our anger fully, then try to reach a thoughtful and a hopeful perspective on the differences we could make.

Marion Cotillard

People who don't take responsibility anger me. And the unequal share of riches and resources. But I believe in forgiveness. When you forgive, you allow yourself to be at peace.

Louise Ridley

Sexism, and yes.

Jody Williams

I'm fuelled by anger against injustice, inequality. If anger makes me get off my ass and do something, then more power to me. I'm not going to hone myself into passivity. One time I was in a serious argument with another Nobel Laureate and I was very angry. The Dalai Lama was close by. Afterward he came over, and I said, "Your Holiness, I'm really sorry, you know, I couldn't help it, I was angry." He just put his hand on me and he said, "Jody, there's nothing wrong with righteous anger. Sometimes, righteous anger is the only right answer." So for all of you who think that anger is wrong, fuck you! That word [fuck] worked its way into the mainstream when the Vietnam War was going on, and became my noun, verb, adjective and adverb, and I've had a lot of trouble reclaiming my full vocabulary. It's a very expressive word.

Forgiveness is a hard one. For example, a very close friend of mine was raped by two men in Spain. They pissed on her and threw her naked into the street. For years, I wanted to go and castrate them, but then I realized that was just putting me on a level with them. But do I forgive them? I doubt it, but I've got past wanting to do anything to them.

“If anger makes me get off my ass and do something, then more power to me. I’m not going to hone myself into passivity.”

JODY WILLIAMS

Tanni Grey-Thompson

Lots of things make me angry, such as people who are cruel to children. There are things that I can forgive and others that I can’t. I have a sliding scale – when people are bitchy or mean, I can deal with it, but there are some things, like cruelty to children, that I find unforgivable.

Paloma Picasso

I actually don’t get angry at all. If I get upset I keep it inside me and don’t show it. Basically, I’m not resentful. I don’t think that resentment cures anything. On the contrary, forgiveness does. It’s best to move on and get on with life – better people, better situations, and just ignore the ones that bother you or hurt you.

“Holding a grudge becomes heavier than the act of forgiveness.”

JUDI DENCH

Judi Dench

Apathy makes me very angry. I hate that attitude of not caring. I don't like people taking things for granted either. And litter makes me terribly angry. In London I walk up some roads and wonder what on earth visitors think when they arrive and see people who live in this place treating it like shit! But I believe in forgiveness. Holding a grudge becomes heavier than the act of forgiveness. It takes a lot of energy out of you. It's like jealousy. If one's very, very jealous it takes such a lot of energy out of you.

DO YOU THINK THERE WILL EVER BE EQUALITY IN HUMANKIND, AN END TO POVERTY AND INJUSTICE? | 4

Maya Angelou

I believe we can achieve all these things, but it will take a very long time. Centuries and centuries. Remember we're the newest group made, we stood up, we remained standing, opposing gravity, we decided not to eat our delicious brothers and sisters but to accord them some right. And then to go further, we tried to love them, whatever that means. That's just in a few million years. Now we have a chance, if we don't kill each other first, to try to strike a balance, try to be a little more good than we are bad.

Ann Leslie

You might get rid of absolute poverty but not relative poverty. For example, the poor in Britain, who have televisions, washing machines, computers, DVDs and mobile phones, are undoubtedly fantastically wealthy compared to people I've seen starving in Africa or North Korea. You could alleviate poverty if you could stop wars. Wars and corruption are the chief causes of poverty in this world, far more so than drought and natural disasters. Democracy helps. The better a country is run, the more accountable it is to its citizens, the more it can alleviate the poverty produced by natural disaster.

Jane Fonda

Even if poverty cannot be eliminated, it can be hugely reduced. For that to be possible, a great deal about human nature needs to change. And I believe that human nature is more determined by social structure or institutions than most people admit. Governments that care for and look after people through their social institutions can help minimize the violence and cynicism and the sense of alienation that so many people have today. This showed up, I thought very interestingly, in Michael Moore's *Bowling for Columbine*, which dealt with violence. Canada, right next to us, has more guns per capita than we do, and Canadians look at the same violent videos, yet they don't lock their doors and they don't have the same problem of violence. I believe it's because their governmental institutions, local and national, take care of people. Not as charity, but in a way that makes them feel worthy.

I always say we don't want band-aids and safety nets, we want trampolines and ladders. Governments that provide trampolines and ladders are going to have citizens that are different. I made a film in Norway called *The Dolphin*, and we used hundreds of local people in some of the scenes. Listening to them and talking to them, I kept thinking there is something about these people, there are no sharp edges, there's a quality of peace about them. I realized it was because of their social structures and the way they are governed.

Yoko Ono

Equality is not what I'm looking for. I would like to see all people achieve their dreams. Dreams may not make them equal.

Kathy Kelly

I think we could reach a point where we would share our resources so that instead of saying, "The poor are always with us," we could actually say, "There shall be no poor among us." We've seen an end to enslavement and can at least say we're not buying and selling human beings as was done in the United States when wealthy estate owners traded slaves as other people might trade stock market portfolios. There are certainly other things that we've seen an end to. We don't any longer see women excluded from voting, and we don't have segregation. Countries like India give me a great deal of hope, really. There is a very vibrant movement to make sure that every Indian child gets a school lunch. And another that insists on at least 100 days of paid labour for every Indian adult of working age.

"Equality is not what I'm looking for. I would like to see all people achieve their dreams. Dreams may not make them equal."

YOKO ONO

Benazir Bhutto

I am an optimist. I've always felt that we human beings can work together and create a better world. Certainly, when the Berlin Wall first came down, I was very excited and thought we would have a peace dividend and all the monies that were being spent on an arms race would be diverted to poverty alleviation. Well, that didn't happen, and now we have entered the age of terrorism. But I still remain convinced that if we work together we can help reduce poverty, we do see that there is a consciousness about the need for the affluent to contribute toward those who are less fortunate. I believe, too, in the case of Pakistan, that by investing in education we can help equip the new generation with ways to have a better life.

Mary McAleese

I start from the absolute principle that we are all equal, that every human being is equal. Now, are we treated equally? That's the difference. I don't think that we are in the process of discovering equality. I think we are in the process of discovering what happens when you fail to treat people equally, how you diminish the whole human family in doing so, and I do believe that we are on a journey. I see the European Union as part and parcel of this journey towards the acknowledgment that the equality and human rights of every human being are absolutely exceptionally important. It's one of the reasons why I'm such a very strong supporter of the concept and the vision at the heart of the European Union. And it's a vision that I think is very shareable throughout the world.

Do I believe that there will be an end to poverty? Yes, I do, because we have all the resources necessary to end those things that diminish the human person. I see what we have been able to achieve in a relatively short time in Ireland. My grandparents lived in a subsistence economy – when electricity came, they didn't get it, because they couldn't figure out they would ever have the money to pay a monthly bill, because they didn't have any kind of income apart from selling the odd cow. So I understand the structure of poverty very well. And yet, bit by bit, we were able to deal with it after we won independence. We are not there yet, but we are much closer in this generation to treating people equally and giving them equal opportunity than we have ever been before. I think every human being would wish that. People in Lesotho or in Honduras are no different: they want the best for their kids. We need to bring our collective imagination, and our will and our sense of responsibility to bear on issues to do with poverty and inequality, and we are beginning to do that.

Jody Williams

Poverty is one of those intractables since time immemorial. I suppose one is supposed to say, "Yes, I believe we will have a perfect world one day." To get to that, we have to stop seeing the world in terms of the individual nation state, and think of the human security of the whole planet, and that takes a huge mind-shift. But that's one of the things I work on, human security, not national security. There's no way on this planet that everybody is going to be equal, that's absurd. I think there's certainly the possibility of justice before the law, people having their basic needs met, housing, education, healthcare, and the right for their children to get a basic education. But how can those basic needs be met when 20% of the planet controls 80% of the resources? Only when people really understand that by giving up a little, you make the whole better. I'd rather have enlightened self-interest than what we have now.

> "What is at stake is your legacy and your children, and if you love your children you have to start thinking in a long-term, sustainable way."
>
> SEVERN CULLIS-SUZUKI

Severn Cullis-Suzuki

There's always going to be injustice. There's always going to be a human side to being human, which means we're not perfect and are always going to be in some kind of a struggle. The forces of good and evil, yin and yang, or whatever you want to call it, are always fighting each other. Right now I think we are at an imbalance where the wealthy nations are destroying and consuming the majority of the world's resources in such a way that the rest of the world is going to suffer. Climate change is a perfect example of that. So there are some major things that absolutely have to be brought into balance. What is at stake is your legacy and your children, and if you love your children you have to start thinking in a long-term, sustainable way. I think we will make the turnaround in terms of ecological sustainability, but I'm worried it's going to come at a massive human cost, because there's still no urgency to do something for the countries that are already suffering from climate change.

Shami Chakrabarti

It depends what you mean by equality. It's hard to imagine perfect equality, but I think it's possible to achieve lesser extremes of wealth and poverty in the world. I don't think we need to see the pictures that we see coming from the developing world – parts of Africa in particular. That's perfectly solvable in my lifetime, or in my son's lifetime. What we lack is political will at a high level, a lack of concerted effort on the parts of governments, and institutions that are even bigger than governments. But I do think there's potential, and I think it's perfectly achievable that there should be much less absolute poverty in the world, much less by way of child death and disease. If you take Britain or Western Europe, it wasn't so many decades ago that you saw child death and disease on an appalling scale, but there has been progress. We don't have a perfect society in Britain, but as far as absolute poverty is concerned, there are no longer any children dying of typhoid on the streets of London. And there's no inherent reason why countries like Britain and other parts of Europe can't take more responsibility for other people's children.

Paloma Picasso

I don't think we can achieve equality and justice for all, though I used to think so when I was younger. We can change the world on a small scale, but from what I've seen, we can't really expect things to get better as a whole. Some people will get better and some people will stay the same or get worse. It's not that I'm pessimistic, I just think that we should do what we can to help others, but not be disappointed if others don't do the same.

Swanee Hunt

Injustice starts out in the human spirit. I think it comes from insecurity. It's like the Jewish saying that I saw in the Holocaust Museum in Washington, something like: "Prejudice is born again in every child." The insecurity that leads to greed is also born again in every child, and the only way to overcome it is to have a wonderfully nurturing, perfect childhood. Sadly, that's just never going to be possible for everyone.

Shirin Ebadi

Of course I dream about people all having the same amount of wealth, but I know that dream cannot come true. What I know *can* come true is the eradication of extreme poverty. More than a billion people in the world live on less than US$1 a day and approximately 80% of the wealth of the world is owned by 1% of the population. The food wasted in the restaurants in the United States and Europe could eradicate hunger. The military budget of the United States has been over $600 billion, and you know what we could do with that amount of money.

Joan Baez

I think there *is* equality in humankind. There probably will not be an end to injustice and poverty, though.

Mary Kayitesi Blewitt

Poverty is relative. You could have everything material and be very rich, but commit suicide because you don't have love. I didn't have anything when I was growing up. We didn't have money, bank accounts or anything, but we were very happy people. So love means everything to me, and I think that warmth, support from relatives, neighbours, these support systems are what matter – you can pull through even if you are homeless and hungry. But worldwide equality? I don't think so. There's too much greed. We all like nice things. It's human nature to compete. I don't necessarily see it as a bad thing, but I think that competition should be healthy. I don't know whether the West really wants to give the developing countries free trade so we can have real competition. That is the concrete thing, and I don't think that's going to happen in my lifetime, to be honest. It will take a long time for Rwanda to get to where America is.

> "Worldwide equality?
> I don't think so.
> There's too much greed."
>
> MARY KAYITESI BLEWITT

Kate Clinton

I need to think that I do believe in equality. Was it Che Guevara who used to say that optimism is the true weapon of the revolutionary? I think I have much more confidence in the innate goodness of people than in the sort of theocracy that I see around me. There is a certain belief that we are born sinful. I don't believe that, so I have faith in people's goodness. I think we are up against the voraciousness of capitalism, which is based on treating certain people as just cogs in a wheel, people not entitled to a fair wage let alone good basic living conditions. Unfortunately, in the last 10 or 15 years we seem to have made inequality a global idea.

Louise Ridley

I don't think we can see a complete end to poverty and injustice, and complete equality of all kinds, no. That's not to say that huge, unimaginable leaps haven't been made in just a few generations – I would recommend the book *Factfulness* by Hans Rosling to everyone as an amazing resource on how the world is a more healthy, equal and safe place than it was just a few decades ago. Stats like how many girls around the world now get an education, and how many people get vaccinations against deadly diseases, are something people consistently underestimate and get wrong in surveys. But it's something the world has to keep working towards and assessing.

> “We are up against the voraciousness of capitalism, which is based on treating certain people as just cogs in a wheel, people not entitled to a fair wage let alone good basic living conditions.”
>
> KATE CLINTON

Tracey Emin

There will never be equality. There will always be poverty and injustice. What mankind should try and do is to attempt to make it less. Achieving fundamental things like health, food, water and especially education would be a great start. I think there are a lot of problems in the world that could be sorted out by education. I opened a library in Uganda and it was fantastic. What is brilliant about Africa is you don't need a lot of money to do something. What you need is initiative, and a good charity that is on the ground level and can get things done. When I was a student at the Royal College of Art, I went round in my lunchtime asking the others to donate pennies and collected about £300 to give to the Red Cross for inoculating children in Sudan. I remember walking off thinking, "Yeah! – that was 600 inoculations." You can do that.

Isabel Allende

I don't think that I or my grandchildren will live to see equality in this world, but we have to aim for it. If we don't start by dreaming of a just world, how are we ever going to achieve it? There was a time when humanity believed that slavery was the only way that hard labour could be done, and few people could envision the end of slavery. But we achieved it – almost. It takes a critical number of people to tip the balance and make profound changes, but it is possible.

Martha Lane Fox

I would love to think there could be an end to these problems, but I honestly don't think it's possible. The huge differences between peoples' environments will always, to a large degree, create economic or other disparities. However, this doesn't mean we shouldn't all be trying to stamp out inequality around us, whether it's racist, sexist, economic or whatever.

Nataša Kandić

I don't believe that people can ever be truly equal. Lots of people work and struggle for a better life for everybody, for food and education for all the world's children. However, I don't see how it could ever be possible for all the people in the world to have the same access to food and justice, and to be free of fear. I don't think that there is enough energy for that, nor perhaps enough will.

Jung Chang

With human nature as it is, it's hard to imagine that true equality and justice could really be achieved throughout the world, but I think there could possibly be an end to poverty one day. Many of us thought that technological and scientific advancement would make poverty history but it hasn't happened yet. However, now that the world is paying more attention, I think that poverty may be solved in the not too distant future. I don't believe injustice can ever end as long as people are as they are.

Wangari Maathai

Whether equality could ever be possible is, I think, a very important question because it means that, before it could happen, humanity would have to look deep into its psyche and decide to understand and embrace the idea of true equality between peoples. A lot of the reasons behind wars are an unwillingness to share or to practise justice and fairness, and that is a very, very common characteristic of human beings everywhere. So we have to learn that it's far better to be fair and just. Selfishness and greed lead to injustices against other human beings and, I would add, against other species as well. Values have to be learned, they don't come to us naturally. We have come a long way as a human family, but we still have a very long way to go.

Mairead Maguire

I believe we can create justice and equality, yes. Since World War II, we have built a body of human rights and laws, the Universal Declaration of Human Rights, to uphold the human dignity of every single man, woman and child on this planet. We have the Women's Movement, the Human Rights Movement, the Fair Trade Movement, the Environmental Movement – I could go on and on. People are saying, "We want a different world. We want equality, justice, and we want to do it non-violently." There is tremendous consciousness among a lot of ordinary people, but unfortunately their voices are not getting through enough to political leaders. And we cannot allow our governments to just set aside these international laws at their whim, endanger the lives of millions and allow the killing we have seen in places like Chechnya, Iraq and Palestine. We have models like Northern Ireland, like South Africa, where people have shown that there is an alternative to militarism and to war, and we want those models to be used.

Tanni Grey-Thompson

I guess I'm an eternal optimist. I think I believe that one day the world will be better and everyone will be equal, because if I didn't believe that, then I'm not sure what would be the point of it all.

Carla Del Ponte

You know, equality is a dream, a dream that I think is almost impossible to achieve. Of course, we must keep working towards equality and continue going in the right direction. We can't just accept the inequalities of our world but must always fight against them. But it's so difficult, and probably will never entirely be achieved. All the same, you must still remain hopeful that full peace will be a reality one day. Many people are criminals, but that doesn't mean we should just give up fighting to prevent crime.

Mary Robinson

We can end injustices if we live up to the commitments of the Universal Declaration of Human Rights. This should be the way in which, as human beings, we order and regulate our lives. I was engaged in harnessing a lot of energies around marking the 60th anniversary of the Universal Declaration in 2008 and trying to bring home the strength of its message: that all human beings are born free and equal in dignity and rights, and that everything else flows from that.

Soledad O'Brien

I'm a realist – I don't have great hopes for injustices ending. But we can put a pretty big dent in poverty if we really try to, and I think people are beginning to want to do this.

Marie Colvin

Our goal can't be to make everybody be like us, but to somehow create a world where people can live the way they really want to. I think there is a possibility of people being able to have their own culture and be different without killing each other. I don't want everybody to be the same. America as the superpower can impose pretty much anything, through force or threats or even brainwashing, but our goal shouldn't be to make everybody else live as we do. It's not about culture or political systems – democracy, communism or whatever. The main thing is that everybody should have access to justice and to the rule of law.

Hanan Ashrawi

I wouldn't say that we can get to this Utopia where everything is fair and lovely. Equality is something you strive for – parity, justice, a sense of fair play. It doesn't mean that you are going to achieve perfect equality, but it's a valid goal and ideal, a tool that can govern and guide your behaviour, your attitude. In a sense, it guides your relationships, the way you make decisions, and the way you view yourself and others and your relationship with others. It becomes a trigger for action against discrimination, exclusion, or disparities, injustices and cruelties. There's a responsibility to remove suffering and to try to make this world a better place in whatever modest ways you can.

> “I can’t stand to see people let themselves be manipulated when they have the freedom not to be – it’s weak and dangerous.”
>
> MARION COTILLARD

Marion Cotillard

I think we are still far from love, sharing and help. I’m a very optimistic person and have faith in humankind, but some days I feel desperate. I hate how some of us rule and manipulate this world, putting money and profit ahead of human issues. I can’t stand to see people let themselves be manipulated when they have the freedom not to be – it’s weak and dangerous.

Christiane Amanpour

I used to believe that everybody’s ideals would lead to equality being realized. But I have come to see that unless a huge, huge proportion of the rich and privileged part of our world decides to end poverty and injustice, it won’t happen. Maybe it will come, but not in my lifetime. It will take a long time.

Dagmar Havlová

I don't think that that we'll ever be able to banish inequality, but it is our duty to try again and again to do it. When you look at history, it is obvious that violence, poverty and injustice have always been there. Unfortunately, they stem from people's negative characteristics, such as vanity, egocentrism and the desire for power.

Mariane Pearl

I don't think there will be a day when we reach a stagnant peace, a form of contentment accessible to most. We are far too complex and contradictory a species. If we want a world of equality, free from misery, and a world of justice, we're going to have to consciously build it. I do believe in the power of individuals to influence the world towards more equality and justice.

Bianca Jagger

We don't seem to be doing the right things to change an economic system that is so unfair – in which the developed world has everything and the developing world lives in such abject poverty. The World Bank, the International Monetary Fund, the World Trade Organization are not there really to find solutions and to have a more equitable world, and therefore I don't know how we will be able to achieve the end of poverty. We won't end poverty simply by rubbing shoulders with heads of states or having a Live Aid concert. What that does is to make millions of people think, "Yes, sure, Bob Geldof and Bono have done this concert, we are going to end poverty and we have found a solution." It's totally absurd that we have found nothing of any real significance.

WHAT IS YOUR GREATEST FEAR? | 5

Ann Leslie

Like most mothers, the only fear that can keep me awake at night is fear for my child. Otherwise, I'm not terribly fearful. Even during wars – and I've worked in war zones a lot – I'm not usually frightened, because adrenalin and the need to get the job done tend to cancel out fear. I only feel frightened in retrospect once the danger has passed. I was never frightened during the Cold War, and I'm not frightened by global warming. Perhaps I should be, but I'm basically a rather sunnily optimistic type of person, and fear is too paralysing and too wasteful of energy. I do, I suppose, fear a helpless old age, locked up in a dismal old people's home, dribbling and being kept alive by tubes. I'd rather drop dead.

Swanee Hunt

The possibility that we will continue responding to the whole idea of terrorism by locking ourselves down more and more really alarms me. I think the response to 9/11 was exactly wrong. We spend billions of dollars every year on airport

> "Like most mothers, the only fear that can keep me awake at night is fear for my child."
>
> ANN LESLIE

security that we could spend educating everyone in the world, every child in the world. That would have been the proper response. Instead, we come up with answers that are very, very short-term positives for some politicians and that may lead to long-term disasters.

Helen Prejean

My greatest fear is that we don't have enough time. I mean time to wake people up and to help change consciousness so that we can protect the planet and begin to have a social fabric of justice and community where everyone has healthcare and housing. The needs of human beings are just so urgent. You can't just hope that the world will change as it needs to. The spirit of Jesus lives on – we didn't come to be served, but to serve.

Shami Chakrabarti

My greatest fear is a country and a world that move backward, that move away from the idea of universal human rights, where everybody is equal in their dignity and worth and entitled to justice. A basic emotional and moral disconnection of that kind could produce an incredible authoritarian, almost totalitarian society, a barbaric society in which any sense of humanity has been lost. That is my worst nightmare – a society or world where the baser instincts – aggression and selfishness – dominate to such an extent that the individual human being no longer matters.

> “Religion is an issue that excites passions very strongly, and unless we can cultivate a culture of tolerance, acceptability and diversity, the danger will be that fanatics will put us on a collision course.”
>
> BENAZIR BHUTTO

Benazir Bhutto

Ever since 9/11 I have worried that some fanatic could trigger another catastrophe that could lead to an estrangement between people of different faiths. Now, not all Muslims are terrorists but, unfortunately, most of the terrorists have been Muslims so this causes a difficulty for most moderate Muslims. Religion is an issue that excites passions very strongly, and unless we can cultivate a culture of tolerance, acceptability and diversity, the danger will be that fanatics will put us on a collision course.

Jane Fonda

My personal fear? Dying with a lot of regrets, when it’s too late to do something about it. When I was sitting next to my father as he died over the course of many weeks and months, I realized that I am not afraid of dying, but I’m terrified of dying with regrets, which I think he did. It made me so sad for him. When I turned 60 I realized, holy shit, this is the third act – the last third of my life. If I want to not have regrets when I die, I've got to deal with it while I'm still young enough to do something about it. I'm dealing with it, but that's my big fear.

Kathy Kelly

The main danger I see is people becoming mesmerized by the complexity and overwhelming cruelty of war as it gets played out in its many different forms, military or economic. It's possible to just become a bit wooden, and that's a very inhumane way for people to respond, I think. A wonderful woman pastor, Dorothee Sölle, had the idea of expressing world suffering and making it tangible and vivid to people through stories or art or photos. To back this up, you need to organize people and circles of activists to deal with tasks and chores that may be very mundane and ordinary – writing articles and press releases to educate people about the issues, sending out emails and organizing non-violence training.

> "My personal fear? Dying with a lot of regrets, when it's too late to do something about it."
>
> JANE FONDA

Mary McAleese

I tend not to be fearful, to be honest. I'm not in the least bit frightened of death or being dead – that doesn't bother me. I think if you've lived in Northern Ireland with death all around you, if you've gone to bed every night as I did for years, waiting for the gunmen to come, waiting for the bombers to come, and they did, and you survived while others didn't, you realize how fickle that all is and just how much luck is in it all. Death is going to happen sometime so I'm prepared for that. I suppose if I have a fear on a personal level, it is that I won't die in my own house. I don't like the idea of being attached to tubes in a strange hospital. Here in Ireland we are pretty much taken with the hospice movement. I'm very hopeful that we can actually give voice to that very strong worry inside all of us that we will be carted off to hospital at a time when we really just want to be left alone to die on our own terms, in our own bed, with our own familiar things around us, in particular with those we love close by us and not a bunch of strangers. It's not so much an overwhelming fear as a kind of a worry that I have.

Bianca Jagger

I fear that we are heading to a climate change disaster faster than we can possibly imagine, and that we are closing our eyes and have not yet decided to confront what we are facing.

Isabel Allende

I fear violence committed with impunity.

Wangari Maathai

I am in fear of what the future holds for many in the poorer countries, especially in those regions that are vulnerable to climate change. We've all seen the terrible devastation created by hurricanes, floods and drought, and the desperate competition for resources in marginal areas.

Judi Dench

The thing I fear most is dying. As a Quaker I should be more resilient about it, but I'm not. We see so many people really suffering badly. When you watch somebody being very, very ill and then dying, you do think it's a kind of release for them, but at the end it's very grim.

Jody Williams

I grew up in the '50s with a real visceral fear of nukes. I now have an intellectual fear of nukes. Nukes could pulverize me, but then you would be gone before you knew it, so it's not the same kind of fear as I had as a kid. But today we see politicians following policies that will lead to another nuclear arms race. Why the hell would you launch another one?

Yoko Ono

I fear to lose freedom by being fearful.

Tanni Grey-Thompson

I fear dying young when I haven't had the chance to do the things that I want to do. When I get to 70 or something, I suppose I won't mind dying but not young. I suppose my biggest fear would be not giving my daughter a good start in life and not being with her when she's in her youth, in those formative years. And I just can't imagine anything worse than one's child being killed.

Paula Rego

I live with a great deal of fear. That's at the core of my being, because it's installed when you are very young. You're afraid of ghosts then, and all sorts of terrifying creatures, and later on you are afraid of fear itself, which can transform itself into acute depression. You're just afraid of fear absolutely. I fear many things.

Kim Phuc

I fear that people do not realize to learn how to live with true love. That is at the root of war, at the root of violence and at the root of people hating ideas and beliefs different from their own. With love we can heal the future.

> “I fear dying young when I haven’t had the chance to do the things that I want to do.”
>
> TANNI GREY-THOMPSON

Soledad O’Brien

I worry for my children. So many young people now lack passion, don’t have anything that moves them – that concerns me. I’m very worried that my children will grow up in a more cynical age. So I hope that they are strong enough to fight cynicism and be who they want to be, and be proud of what kind of voice they may have. I hope they’ll also have a certain amount of faith. I think that’s really important in developing who you are and what kind of person you become.

Carla Del Ponte

I have no fear – I am always an optimist. I do see the dangers and the reality of the world today, but I am also a fatalist, so fear doesn’t really come into my philosophy. Fear of what? You cannot live with fear because it weakens you. Of course, dangers exist, but we must accept risks because they are a part of life. We all have to do our best and accept that the fight is never-ending.

Mairead Maguire

My concern is that people might not recognize their own power to make a difference. That we might not recognize the tremendous things that are happening in our world today, and the great advances we are making in our progression towards a better society.

Hanan Ashrawi

I fear for those I love. Healthy fear can be a means of self-preservation and an active way to get my loved ones all the protection and security that I can. But I don't allow unhealthy fear to take over, as it can cause paralysis, inaction. Fear has motivated me not to take stupid risks, but I never allowed it to stop me from taking action. My belief that I was doing the right thing has helped me to cope with my fear; the sense that I'm doing something of value, that I can make a difference. You find the proper place for fear, for healthy fear, and you cope with it because you know that you cannot be a bystander, you cannot be a passive victim. You have to be an active agent of change.

Paloma Picasso

Fear is not a sentiment that I like to have, so I move on to doing something about it, and I think that's the best way to react. I believe that fear is something you create yourself.

> “My concern is that people might not recognize their own power to make a difference.”
>
> MAIREAD MAGUIRE

Mary Robinson

I'm afraid that the trend towards global warming will actually take us beyond the tipping point, and that the world of my grandchildren will be an even harsher and less secure one than it is for most people today.

Sinéad O'Connor

My greatest fear is that a paedophile might abduct a child of mine, and my next greatest fear is that my children might be connected with drugs.

Maya Angelou

Oh, I wouldn't mention fear. Oh no! And lose some power? I try not to give the negatives any power. You see, my son, my only son, was in an automobile accident when he was 17 and had his neck broken. He has since lived through that and another accident, and was paralysed from the neck down and told he would never walk again. He had the same vertebrae crushed as Christopher Reeve had. And now he walks.

Mary Kayitesi Blewitt

My real concerns are about my children. I think we adults have let them down. Some of the things we're doing will have a harmful impact on their lives in the future. We see young people attacking older people on the street, or behaving in other ways we'd never have dreamt of in our generation. It's a reflection on what is happening to our society. So that makes me frightened when I look at my kids and think that it doesn't matter how much you educate them, it doesn't matter how much faith, love or careful upbringing you give them, the world out there is not a good one.

Jung Chang

One of my biggest fears is the repeat of another century like the last one when tyrants like Hitler, Stalin and Mao did so much damage to humankind. I'm so afraid that that scenario might happen again.

Martha Lane Fox

I've overcome a lot of my fears since nearly dying in a really horrific car crash. My fears have always been very personal, and I think my biggest one is just that I'll let myself, or those around me, down. I beat myself up a lot and think, have I done enough? Am I thinking enough? Am I working hard enough? Am I doing enough good? Am I being creative enough? Am I busy enough?

Kate Clinton

Fear can be on a mundane level. For example, if something horrible were to happen and my girlfriend was, say, in San Francisco and I was in New Jersey, we might be unable to get back together. After 9/11 the moments when you say goodbye have been transformed. A lot of women and people of colour and poor people live and endure a kind of daily fear. But before 9/11 the white guys who were running the country at the time had never been terrorized. They didn't react well – they overreacted completely in the wrong direction. "We were attacked by Saudi Arabians so let's invade Iraq!" Now we have a kind of global, generalized fear.

Christiane Amanpour

My biggest worry is that there won't be an end to poverty and injustice, and that the distorted world we live in will become more and more dangerously unbalanced, more and more divided between rich and poor.

Shirin Ebadi

I fear civil war – brothers killing brothers. When there is a foreign enemy, you know what you have to do – you have to defend yourself. But when there is a civil war, then people who knew each other and were friends or neighbours start pulling out guns and killing each other.

Marie Colvin

I fear testing my abilities and finding that I'm not good enough. But it does make me go on trying to get it right and bear witness to matters that are more important than my individual life, or whether my wisteria is growing!

Louise Ridley

In terms of phobias, heights are not for me, but I like to think I don't have a "greatest fear". If something scares you a little it often means you should have a go at it.

Marion Cotillard

I fear our madness regarding the destruction of the earth and then of ourselves. The fact that some animals are losing their reference marks (migrating birds, for example). The accelerated disappearance of species and forests.

> "I fear our madness regarding the destruction of the earth and then of ourselves."
>
> MARION COTILLARD

Dagmar Havlová

Apart from my fear for the health of my nearest and dearest, I worry about whether I will have enough strength and energy to complete all the things that I have promised I will do in this lifetime. Things like setting up the Václav Havel Library, which was a kind of pioneering task in the Czech Republic. I have fear for the planet we live on and the way we are devastating it for the generations to come. I fear that one day we'll all have to wear an electronic chip that will monitor us. That the energy of human dialogue will lapse and all communication will be based on cold machines.

Nataša Kandić

My only fear comes from my belief that nothing has changed in the former Yugoslavia. I expected that after the war, the truth would come out and justice would be done, that Serbs would take responsibility for what happened. Now I fear that the whole truth will never be known, that victims will never see justice done, and in the future, perhaps in 15 years, a new generation could go through the same terrible experiences.

WHICH WOMAN OR WOMEN, PAST OR PRESENT, DO YOU MOST ADMIRE? | 6

Judi Dench

I admired Peggy Ashcroft very much indeed. So many things happened to her during her life, and her vulnerability, resilience and spirit were just wonderful. And I admire Marjorie Wallace. I admire people who go out on a limb, to pursue a dream that they have. Most of these are men, but I do admire lots of women.

Ann Leslie

I admired Mrs Thatcher enormously. As a woman she was automatically an outsider in the masculine world of British politics – and especially in the Tory party – so she thought outside the conventions of the male club. In the end, she terrified the men who'd initially patronized her. In history, one of my favourite women role models is the 19th-century explorer Mary Kingsley. In Africa she lived with cannibal tribes and endured – with great humour – enormous travails and dangers. It's amazing. She always dressed as if she was at a Victorian tea party in a big skirt and buttoned-up blouse, with boots and a parasol. She became a huge celebrity in Victorian Britain and published one of the funniest and most moving books I have ever read: *Travels in West Africa*. She went to South Africa to become a nurse during the Boer War and died from disease relatively young. Her courage, her humour and her refusal to let gender or convention stand in her way are terrifically inspiring.

Marion Cotillard

I discovered Aung San Suu Kyi when my mother took me to see John Boorman's movie *Beyond Rangoon*. I was 19 and knew nothing of Burma, but from that day on she has been my hero. Another is Mariane Pearl, an amazingly beautiful soul. And Shirin Ebadi. I read her very interesting book *Iran Awakening* some years ago, and it tells us a lot about the world and how politics and manipulation work.

Sinéad O'Connor

My biggest female hero would be Harriet Tubman – the tiny, ordinary, granny kind of woman who organized and ran the secret escape route nicknamed the "Underground Railroad", for smuggling slaves from the south of America into the north just before the American Civil War. By finding people who would give them help and shelter along the way, she managed to rescue hundreds of families and people from slavery. I guess my next biggest hero would be Joan of Arc. I admire her for the female warrior force that she was.

> "I admire people who go out on a limb, to pursue a dream that they have."
>
> JUDI DENCH

Kate Clinton

One of the lovely things about living in New York City is that you really get to meet people that you admire. I admire Gloria Steinem, I think she is really an American saint, though she would kill me for saying this about her. She once mentioned about that draconian Supreme Court decision that basically continues to support the ban on late term partial birth abortion, and which just continues the chipping away at every woman's right to choose. I was so upset about it, but Gloria goes on steadily, working for her foundation that helps needy women's organizations. So I really do admire her, not only for her intelligence and clarity but also for her wicked sense of humour. I'm also very inspired by the work of my girlfriend, Urvashi Vaid. She is very much an activist who began working for the American Civil Liberties Union in prison reform. She's been very active in the Gay and Lesbian movement. She has tremendous energy.

Joan Baez

Mothers are the admirable ones. When you ask a woman what she does, it means, "What do you do out in the world? Are you only a homemaker? What are your hobbies?" She doesn't have time for that. A mother's role is all-consuming, but at least now the work at home and responsibility are beginning to be shared by fathers.

> “Mothers are the admirable ones.”
>
> JOAN BAEZ

Jane Fonda

Eleanor Roosevelt I admired a lot. But the women I admire most are people like Lois Gibbs, a shy retiring homemaker in Love Canal outside of Buffalo. Her community realized that it was built on a toxic dump when their children began to be born with birth defects and die from cancer. Lois turned her anger into activism by founding a national organization to stop toxic waste. She remains to this day a national leader. I'm always in awe of these working-class women who become real leaders, and I've had the privilege to meet many of them.

Jody Williams

Shirin Ebadi is one of my closest Nobel Laureate women friends. She and I created this Nobel Women's Initiative together, and I think she is wonderful. But who really inspire me are women who work tirelessly to make the world better and nobody knows who they are. There are so many of them in the world. It's women who bust their butts to make the world better while men are making war and conflict.

Tracey Emin

When I was younger, I used to quite like the idea of Lady Hamilton. She was really smart. She started when she was 13 living this kind of questionable life and she turned it all around, she is a really good role model. And Bess of Hardwick who started the first British banking system that had only a low rate of interest for the people on her land – women in history who actually changed things. I admire the artist Louise Bourgeois.

Tanni Grey-Thompson

I admire my mother because she was such a strong woman. She made positive choices and didn't let other people's perception of me stand in the way of the belief she gave me. She was very strong and quite stroppy – I'm turning into her! I had a wonderful deputy headmistress in high school, Audrey Jones, who was a feminist. She was very keen on encouraging women to be engineers, for example, and not just stay within the norms of the time. When I was growing up I never thought, "I can't do this, because I'm disabled and female." Of course, there were, and are, many things I can't do, but I always start off thinking I can.

Maya Angelou

I admire my grandmother and my mother, who was very different. And my "chosen sister", Coretta Scott King, who believed non-violent protest could awaken a nation dozing in its history of slavery.

Swanee Hunt

Eleanor Roosevelt is probably the woman I most admire. She had a very tough time for many reasons, including feeling unattractive and finding out that her husband was having an affair with the nanny. Yet she stayed married to him and rose above her personal anguish to care about the world. She was brilliant, and she was one of the founders of the League of Women Voters.

Mairead Maguire

As a young woman in Belfast, I remember admiring Dorothy Day who started the Catholic Worker Movement in America, where she opened shelters for the homeless, the poor. She was one of the very first women who talked about non-violent protest against war, against nuclear weapons, and for international rights, human rights. She called on people to serve the poor, and she lived that out fully in her own life.

Paloma Picasso

Well, I admire my mother, for sure. She is a very impressive woman. When I was about 13 and started to hear people talking about women's liberation, I thought, what are they talking about? Because of course, I already had what people were looking for at home – a woman who took things into her own hands and raised her kids on her own, believing that there is no difference, basically, between what a man can do and a woman can do if they set their mind to it.

Helen Prejean

Among the early women saints and mystics in the Church I admire Teresa of Avalon, who reformed her religious community, and Julian of Norwich, who experienced close intimacy with God and spread her wisdom by counselling people from a little anchorite cell in her church. In the Bible, Mary is often pictured as a blue and white Madonna on a pedestal, way above the human race, but she was a 13- or 14-year-old Palestinian girl when she had Jesus, and she lived in poverty. I think she was a woman of her time and had to grow into understanding what Jesus talked about. I see her as a model of discipleship.

“Mary is often pictured as a blue and white Madonna on a pedestal, way above the human race ... I think she was a woman of her time.”

HELEN PREJEAN

Wangari Maathai

I very much admired my mother and later on many other beautiful women like Margaret Mead, and Mother Teresa. There's a common thread running through them. They were all women who were working beyond their own lives, never looking for something for themselves.

Carla Del Ponte

For me, Margaret Thatcher was an absolutely strong woman who could do a lot. I was very impressed with her book. I also greatly admired Golda Meir. I have met many women politicians who are dealing with important issues, and I think that women are much better than men at using power, because they keep their feet on the ground. I also believe strongly in women's intuition. I admire Micheline Calmy-Rey, who was head of the Swiss Federal Department of Foreign Affairs, and many other women in Swiss politics.

Mary Robinson

I admire, and very often quote, Eleanor Roosevelt, because of her role in relation to the Universal Declaration of Human Rights. But more generally, I've always admired women at the grassroots level. In the Irish context, I think of those who have made a difference in very difficult circumstances. In Africa, I'm impressed by women at many different levels. Women like Graça Machel who has become a good friend. Women I met recently in Ghana, who came to see me to talk about the struggle in which they were engaged. Women who are fighting gender-based violence, and also some of the human rights defenders that I met during my time as UN High Commissioner, including brave Pakistani women like Hina Jilani.

Bianca Jagger

Eleanor Roosevelt has been a real role model for me. And so has my mother, who believed in women's emancipation at a time when most women solely devoted themselves to home-making and were regarded as second-class citizens. I always feel sad that we still live in a society where there is a concerted effort to make heroes out of men and not out of women.

Mary McAleese

The woman most inspirational to me growing up was Catherine of Siena, without a doubt. What I particularly like about her is her fidelity to what she believed in and her ability to speak with startling courage and clarity. Over my lifetime, I have become very drawn to her, drawn more deeply into her writings. She was illiterate, and her writings that are so strong and powerful were dictated. I'm sad to say that she was one of only two female Doctors of the Church, I wish there had been more in the Church that I happen to belong to.

The other person, in contemporary times, who has most inspired me is Anne Maguire, mother of the famous Maguire family who were prosecuted in London for conspiracy to bomb. There was no evidence against them whatsoever, yet unfortunately the system, the media, the courts, the judiciary, the police, and indeed the world of forensic science, were so obsessed with the threat from terrorism that it blinded them to the truth. She spent ten years in prison. It devastated her family, her two sons who spent time in prison for nothing, and her husband. He spent time in prison too, and it broke his spirit. It never, ever broke Anne's spirit, and it has never stopped her from forgiving. There is a radiance about that woman, the most lovely person I have ever met in my life. Every time I feel even remotely threatened with a dose of self-pity, I just think of her and say to myself, "Would you ever shut up!"

Nataša Kandić

I've met many ordinary people who for me are heroes, people who have tried to do whatever they could do for others, and few of them are famous. I do admire Carla Del Ponte who was the main prosecutor in the international criminal tribunals. She accused Milošević, Karadžić, Mladić, and I see her as a woman with integrity and strength, with great empathy for the victims of war crimes.

Martha Lane Fox

I admire lots of women. I studied ancient and modern history, and I think one of the women who always fascinated me was Emperor Justinian's wife, Helen. She ran his empire while he was charging around trying to expand it in lots of different directions. She was a very interesting woman and a strong character – one of the first empresses to wield some real clout back in about 500 AD. I've had the privilege of working with an organization called CAMFED, which supports female education in Africa and is working to overcome AIDS and change the economic dynamics there. Through that, I've met some astonishing women who've literally dragged themselves out of the most terrible situations and created their own businesses, set up schools or changed their local village's fortunes in a host of ways. I've taken a great deal of inspiration from women in that programme.

Kathy Kelly

I greatly admire Barbara Deming because of her life and witness, and her philosophy, published as *We are All Part of One Another*. She was very much a part of the early non-violent Civil Rights movement in the United States.

Mariane Pearl

Many of the women who inspire me are hard-working and anonymous. Like Fatima Elayoubi, a Moroccan cleaner who lives in a Paris suburb. She was illiterate, but she wrote a book of poetry phonetically, called *Prayer to the Moon*. Her book, later transcribed into French, talks about being unnoticed. Going through entire days cleaning up people's homes without meeting anyone who bothers to acknowledge your presence or to give you legitimacy. I also have female friends who inspire me too. As did my mother, and as does the writer Toni Morrison.

Severn Cullis-Suzuki

I admire many of the women you've interviewed for this book, such as Wangari Maathai. But I would have to say my biggest role model is my mother during my whole life, I can think of so many examples where she just rolled up her sleeves and did something about what she disagreed with. There have been so many projects that my mum's worked on that demonstrate that you can change society.

Louise Ridley

It's hard to pick one but at the forefront of my mind as I write this is Monica Lewinsky. The international shaming and abuse she went through, which never would have happened had her affair with Bill Clinton taken place today, was hideous and completely unfair. It shows the distance we've come in terms of understanding sexual politics that many people now rightly think that Donald Trump talking about "grabbing women by the pussy" is not okay. The fact that Lewinsky has come through her experience, told her story and now works to prevent online bullying, in the full knowledge that to millions of people she'll never not be "that woman", is very inspiring.

Mary Kayitesi Blewitt

Every woman, to me, is a hero. Those that get to the top are lucky to be there, but there are many who do so much that is not recognized, least of all by men. They all deserve an award.

Kim Phuc

I admire my mum. The one who had me, the one who loved me, the one who stood by me. She showed me that with little things we can make a difference. We don't need to be somebody big to make a big difference.

> “Every woman, to me, is a hero.”
>
> MARY KAYITESI BLEWITT

Dagmar Havlová

I admire the women who took care of the wounded in hospitals during wars and displayed exceptional courage and determination while knowing that they could not change much. There was such despair, but they still tried to care for and save others. I also admire women who care for old people who are bedridden or in hospices. They do the work of children who should be looking after their parents, because it is our obligation to look after our parents' generation.

Marie Colvin

I admire Martha Gellhorn, Hemingway's third wife, herself an absolutely wonderful writer. I take her book on the Spanish Civil War with me to whatever war I happen to be covering. She wrote with purity, clarity and ferociousness. Because I work in and care about the Middle East, I also admire someone like Gertrude Bell, who came from a very traditional English background, yet went off and changed the Middle East in a non-showy way.

Christiane Amanpour

I most admire Marie Curie, Margot Fonteyn, Martha Gellhorn, Oriana Fallaci and Gloria Steinem.

Emma Bonino

Among present women, I certainly admire Aung San Suu Kyi, but also lesser-known women like Somaly Mam, who fights against women's exploitation in Cambodia, and Khady Koita, from Senegal, who campaigns against female genital mutilation. They both wrote books about their experience: chilling accounts of women's condition.

Benazir Bhutto

I was studying in England when Mrs Thatcher was made Leader of the Opposition, and even though my political views were different from hers, I always had a great admiration and respect for her, and for the fact that she had made it in a man's world. But as a young Muslim woman, my role model was Bibi Khadija, the first wife of the Prophet of Islam. I always used to tell people that the Prophet married a working woman, and that God chose Bibi Khadija to be the first one to give witness to Islam. That meant that God thought women were very important. Bibi Khadija was a businesswoman with her own caravans for trading goods, and while the Prophet was married to her he only had one wife. She was older than him, and after she died the Prophet married several women, one of whom, Ayesha, actually participated in a war. So I found it very difficult to accept that Muslim women should be confined to the four walls of their home or to the all-enveloping black veil, given that the noblest women leaders of Islam, the wives of the Prophet, were working women.

In Arabia before Islam came, there was a tribal society and people did not want girl children. They would often bury a girl child alive. The Prophet of Islam stopped that. He said, "All are equal before the eyes of God." So if all are equal before the eyes of God, why should women be subjugated? The fact that the Prophet stopped the murder of girl children made me a very strong believer that people who commit domestic violence, or any violent attack against women, must be punished. I have seen in this new generation that the interpretations of Islam have somehow been changed by a new generation of Islamic scholars. For me Islam came as a religion of emancipation and liberation. Where in the Koran is it written that women are supposed to cover themselves from head to foot?

"I admire strong, loving, assertive and independent women of all ages and in all times."

ISABEL ALLENDE

Isabel Allende

I admire strong, loving, assertive and independent women of all ages and in all times.

Shami Chakrabarti

In Britain, I think Helena Kennedy is a great role model for all young campaigning lawyers. Further back, I admire the suffragettes, so many women who campaigned for the cause of women, but also the cause of humankind. One has to give a great deal of credit to Eleanor Roosevelt for being one of the greatest architects of what we now believe human rights to be: the post-war human rights settlement. A remarkable achievement. Some modern politicians that come up against organizations like mine think that we're somehow stuck in the past, because we celebrate the post-1945 settlement. They think it's somehow reactionary and not modern to be harking back to that period in history: post-Holocaust, post Blitz, where people of all political persuasions, people of all the great world religions, and people with no religion, came together and settled on certain principles that are essential to the preservation of democracy and the preservation of human dignity.

Eleanor Roosevelt played a remarkable part in that, not a politician herself, not a great jurist herself, but someone who just had the vision and the skills to help achieve that settlement, someone who also understood that human rights

> “Eleanor Roosevelt was a visionary, whose legacy is probably greater than that of many far more famous world leaders – mostly men.”
>
> SHAMI CHAKRABARTI

are not just legal instruments – not just about treaties and laws, but they are actually, as she said, to be found in the small places close to home. Places so small that they can't be found on any map of the world. She was a visionary, whose legacy is probably greater than that of many, far more famous world leaders – mostly men. That legacy is something we're desperately trying to hold on to, because it's under attack at times. Not just in Britain or in Europe, but all over the world, where people think that one should replace these hard-won rights and freedoms and values by making exceptions to deal with particular threats, such as terrorism or even economic threats. In other words, that the rules of the game should change and we should keep reinventing society in a way that is ultimately destructive to society's core.

Yoko Ono

I admire all women.

Hanan Ashrawi

I'm always quite eclectic. I never say there is one model or one person, or one incident. I find what is good in different people, in different women, and these things influence me, most of the time in very subtle ways. They don't have to be dramatic or conscious even. Some events or individuals have a greater impact than others, and you absorb them into your own sense of values and into your lifestyle and choices. I mainly admire the women I know, more than historical figures. Most of them I look at as friends – for instance Anna Lindh, the Swedish Foreign Minister who was assassinated, was a good friend of mine.

7

DO YOU THINK WOMEN CAN MAKE A DIFFERENCE IN THE WORLD AND BE INSTRUMENTAL IN STOPPING WAR?

Kate Clinton

It's time men stepped aside and let women show what they can do. Give us a chance, for goodness' sake! I find the level of sexism in the US unbelievable. If I had a dollar for every time I've said this, I could buy my own Senator. I mean the conversation that went on about a woman running for President. And the fact that we only have three women out of nine justices in the Supreme Court. In my travels, I find so many women doing amazing, unheralded, really creative work in their communities. As always, that will be where the revolution starts.

Kathy Kelly

I don't go along with the idea that women have a purer vision of a world without war. It doesn't seem to play out that way at all. Women, as much as men, should take responsibility for having in one way or another accommodated the idea of war. We've raised children who somehow aren't brave enough to involve themselves in the hard work of campaigning to get rid of weapons and to say, "We will no longer tolerate the threat of force." We all face some very hard questions. Why do we believe we should be protected by people using threats and force in our name? All those involved in raising children, whether they're teachers, or parents, or care-givers in some capacity, or whether they create television shows, or movies, or pop culture have a deep responsibility to do something about this issue. We all do.

Swanee Hunt

I spend two-thirds of my time working on the woman's role in preventing war. We've sponsored research in 15 places where women were involved in the demobilization of soldiers, in reform of security forces or in the actual prevention of a conflict. Women are tremendously influential in their families, as well as in the community, and when they organize and get together, they can do remarkable things. A group of women surrounded a building in Ghana where a meeting was being held with warlords from Liberia, and they wouldn't let the warlords out of the building until they'd come to a peace agreement. In Russia, some women organized a committee of soldiers' mothers who confronted Russian generals and got their 18-year-old sons pulled out of the barracks. According to the American Ambassador to Russia, their efforts led to the end of the first Chechen war.

Mary McAleese

I am putting a lot of my faith in women, because we are really only at the beginning, aren't we, of women's journey into the places of power and influence in the world? It's only a century ago that they were still fighting for the right to vote. It's hard for our children and our girls in particular to believe that. It's only 100 years ago that the university that I worked in for a good deal of my life, Trinity College here in Dublin, got round to letting women through its doors. In human terms, it's not

> "I think we have been living in a world that has been flying on one wing when we were given two."
>
> MARY MCALEESE

a lot of time. It is worth remembering that the suffragettes were called terrorists, and the government at the time said it would never negotiate with terrorists. We forget these stories so quickly. Now we have Equal Opportunities legislation that we never had before. We have a growing consciousness of the worth of women. We see it, for example, here in Ireland where we have prosperity undreamt-of a generation ago, and one of the reasons is that we have 300,000 more women in the workplace now than we had 20 years ago. Their genius is now flooding into places it never had the chance to reach in the past.

Now it's still evident if you look at the world of politics, of theology, of business, of industry, that we are still awaiting the full revelation of the power, the genius and the special charisma of women. It is my hope that it will counter the culture of machismo for which we have paid such a revolting price in the last century, particularly in terms of wars. I'm not saying that men are exclusively driven by machismo urges or violence. I don't believe that to be true, but I believe that the voices of men who believe passionately in peace really need the vindication and the authentication that comes from the voices of women making the same point. I think we have been living in a world that has been flying on one wing when we were given two. In the places where education and the liberation of women are beginning to have an impact, we see ourselves becoming better at solving problems in more imaginative and less conflict-driven ways.

Let's get women into the places where their potential and their genius can make a huge difference. I was lucky that the opportunities were beginning to arise, the cracks were beginning to open, and there were spaces that we could colonize as women. My daughters have even more space, and their daughters in turn will have more space again, so it's my hope that there is a generation coming whose landscape will be one of full equality and equal treatment. I think that would be a brilliant world. I hope I'm around to see it and not too gaga to appreciate it!

Ann Leslie

It's something of a feminist myth that women are inherently more peaceable creatures. There have always been women in history who were very tough, very ambitious, and went to war with great enthusiasm. Boudicca, Elizabeth I, the Rani of Jhansi, Golda Meir, Mrs Thatcher and Mrs Gandhi were no softies. The Prophet Mohammed's favourite wife,

Ayesha, rode a camel into battle. And I've met several murderous women in war zones like Zimbabwe and the former Yugoslavia. On the other hand, women have children, and that does tend to put a brake on them. But the idea that if the world were run by women, all would be sweetness and light under a loving sisterhood is frankly sentimental nonsense. Power is not only an aphrodisiac, as Henry Kissinger put it, but it always changes people who acquire it. Women who get it, and who want to hang on to it, tend to behave just like men.

Jane Fonda

I think it will be and has to be women who lead the way – partly because we have less to lose in trying to change the status quo. There's a saying that "Women and girls are the agents of change." I made a documentary called *Generation 2000* about girls' programmes in Nigeria, and what feminists there discovered is that it's important to work with young girls before they have internalized social gender stereotypes. That's where you create leaders who will take us into change. You have to start with girls of 12 to 14, who will then help older women reclaim the voices that they lost as adolescents.

Benazir Bhutto

Women are critical in stopping war. I think the first generation of liberated women felt that they had to prove they were equal to men. I know that when I was first elected Prime Minister, I was so much on the defensive that I felt that I had to be as tough as a man to prove that I was equal to a man and up to the job. Then as I started working, I found that people just actually wanted someone who would take care of them and their families. Somebody who was going to take note of their anxieties, their problems, and find solutions. I think the reason why so many Eastern women leaders have come forward is because, in the East, there is that yearning for a maternal figure, somebody who sees the rest of society as her children. So the real issues are those that pertain to health, education, drinking water, transport and the general facilitating of day-to-day life.

Women give birth to life. So I think that women have a moderating influence and that it's very important for us to involve them in decision-making. If there are more women leaders, more women in parliament and more women in the workforce, societies will moderate – as long as the women don't then become like men, but I don't think that will happen. As people, the sexes have a lot of similarities, but there are also crucial differences. One of them is that men tend to be more assertive and women tend to be more conciliatory or try to find the middle way.

Paloma Picasso

I believe that women are more caring and respectful of life because they create life more directly and care for their babies in a closer way than men do. I think that women may be able to make some changes to the world, but the nature of mankind is still violent. We all have some of that in us. Women tend to look at things in a more conservative and protective way. Wars are still going to happen, but women could maybe work to stop them being so long or so cruel, especially to non-belligerents.

Jody Williams

Well, if you want to take the example of the landmine campaign, it is primarily women who really run it. I was the founding Coordinator from late 1991 until February of 1998; Liz Bernstein took over then and was Coordinator until 2004, and many of the people around the Coordinators are women. There are certainly good men, my husband and his organization single-handedly, with the ICRC, banned blinding laser weapons. But it's women who have been really instrumental in moving the landmine issue forward, just as they are in peace and human rights movements.

Isabel Allende

Women make up 51% of humanity but this is not reflected in the management of the world. Men make most of the decisions. Women do two-thirds of the labour, yet they own less than 1% of the world assets. Women and children are collateral damage in times of war and also in times of peace. A critical number of women in positions of power, nurturing the feminine energy in men, will change the world and bring peace.

Mariane Pearl

From what I have witnessed, women are the most vital agents for change. Women mostly do not believe in wars, but they believe in education. They believe in allowing life to grow. They would rather die than deprive their children of education. And sometimes they do die. Many women in the world, in Africa and Asia, are extremely humbling to me. Their strength and courage, what they can teach us about resilience, is probably our best asset to build peace.

> “Women can make a difference. The problem is that by the time they get into a position of power to do it, they have changed.”
>
> JOAN BAEZ

Paula Rego

Women can make all the difference in the world if they put their mind to it. It's good to be organized in some way, though it's very difficult to do it on your own. For instance, I tried to make a difference in Portugal where the Catholic Church forbids making abortion more accessible. I knew the suffering this caused and therefore I did a series of pictures on girls having abortions, most of them teenage girls, schoolgirls. There have been two referendums on the issue, and in the first one, women didn't bother to go and vote. In the second one, they did, and I must say I'm very proud that newspapers used my pictures as propaganda. You do what you can.

Joan Baez

Yes, women can make a difference. The problem is that by the time they get into a position of power to do it, they have changed – I mean Hillary Clinton would make a good man. They are afraid they wouldn't get elected if they didn't change – and they probably wouldn't.

Marion Cotillard

The power of women to make a difference is huge. Look at Aung San Suu Kyi, Mariane Pearl, Shirin Ebadi and more: Mother Teresa, Jane Addams, Wangari Maathai, Simone Weil, Eve Ensler ... There's still a long way to go but the voice of women is being taken more and more seriously.

Helen Prejean

We see women working together to make a difference all the time. It's not by accident that the UN said that the way to lift all people up is to lift up the women. They are the educators, the ones in constant touch with family and children. A group that works worldwide giving micro-loans to start small businesses has said that the percentage of women who return those loans is something like 95% because women work in community. They know they can't go it alone.

Tanni Grey-Thompson

Women can make a difference because they have a different point of view. That's a gross generalization, but I still think there's a different mindset. For me, war is the absolute, final horror. It would never be even on my radar to think, "Let's go and fight somebody."

Louise Ridley

Absolutely – though so can men. I used to believe that if women ran the world it would be a less violent place, but reading *The Power* by Naomi Alderman changed that view. In her book, women become physically stronger than men and that starts to change the power balance in society. It made me realize that whoever has power – any kind of power – is at risk of abusing it.

Sinéad O'Connor

I think that the biggest way in which women can stop wars or influence the world is by raising their children with proper values. Ultimately, it comes down to what values are taught to the children who are going to be men in the future.

Nataša Kandić

Women in war are much stronger at fighting for truth and justice. In Sierra Leone, in Rwanda, in former Yugoslavia, I heard women's voices against war crimes. It's men who make war, weapons have always been in the hands of men. Afterward only women have the courage to tell the truth about what has happened. Men try to cover up their participation in war crimes. Women are fighters for betterment, truth and justice. Men are mostly fighters for power.

Martha Lane Fox

Women can absolutely make a difference and are already instrumental in opposing war. It's easy for someone like me to forget how recent the women's equality movement is. True equality may take a long time but I think it will continue to expand across the whole world, not just in the wealthy West. The more women who become politicians, presidents, prime ministers and holders of other high offices, the more we'll see them changing the mechanisms of politics and power. Their influence is only just beginning to be felt.

> “Women are fighters for betterment, truth and justice. Men are mostly fighters for power.”
>
> NATAŠA KANDIĆ

Emma Bonino

Women are generally seen as less war-prone than men. I am not a sociologist of course, but I'm not too convinced about this – there are many examples around the world of women in power who can hardly be defined as non-violent. The truth is that women have never had sufficient power to demonstrate where they stand. For me, above all, women are not a "category" per se, to be defined one way or the other. I hope, actually, that their empowerment will bring about the notion of individuality as a value, versus the notion of categories.

Shirin Ebadi

Women can have the most important role in preventing wars, both as citizens and as people who can influence their husbands, their sons and their brothers who are fighting wars. It's important to remember that it is not only governments who decide about war and peace: the people of the world can influence such issues.

> "Women bring deep compassion and the understanding that human life is sacred."
>
> MAIREAD MAGUIRE

Judi Dench

I definitely think women can make a difference. I think that we look at things in a totally different way to men, and have an entirely different comprehension of the way things are. That's not to say it's necessarily better or worse, but it's different, perhaps a softer side.

Mairead Maguire

Women can certainly make a difference in the world, and be models of peacemaking and conflict resolution. Here in Northern Ireland in 1976 when we started the Peace People, we were on the brink of civil war, no one really knew where to turn or what to do. And when we called for people to come out and march and mobilize for peace, 90% of the people who marched in their hundreds of thousands throughout Northern Ireland and elsewhere were women. Women bring a sense of consensus to their work. They also bring deep compassion and the understanding that human life is sacred.

Shami Chakrabarti

Of course, women can make a difference in all sorts of ways. If our political structures better reflected our society – most obviously, if there were more women in them – I think we would have a better world. If you're talking about wars, it's very obvious to me that women and children suffer the most. Like most rational people I would like to see less war in the world, but faced with Hitler in the last century, I wouldn't have spoken against World War II. Sometimes people have to go to war, so I am not a pacifist. But perhaps when politics and governments have a greater portion of women in them, wars will be less likely because the human cost would be more weightily measured than it sometimes is at the moment. War would become much more a measure of last resort.

Jung Chang

I don't think women themselves can make a decisive difference, but we can all contribute in some way.

"If you're talking about wars, it's very obvious to me that women and children suffer the most."

SHAMI CHAKRABARTI

Marie Colvin

Everybody has a responsibility to try to make a difference in a very difficult world. People do listen less to women, but women could change this by being more confident in themselves as individuals. I think the question of gender is important and integral to who you are, and you can't deny that women and men are different. I think fundamentally that every single experience in our lives affects us whether we are men or women. Obviously someone like me has more of a voice. I don't buy into the theory that if women ran the world, it would be a better place. Margaret Thatcher was a woman, and she went to war! She seems to me to have been an example of a woman who thought the only way to deal with the world was to take on what are perceived as traditional male values, like strength and power. I don't think all men are like that. I think women can be, and have been, strong leaders in many different ways.

Dagmar Havlová

Both sexes should try to be instrumental in stopping war. There are women who have personified this ideal, and also women who have provoked wars or been the cause of them. Part of Czech mythology was the so-called "Girls' War" when women got together and used sex to outsmart men. Yes, and if a man succumbed, they killed him. They simply revolted against male supremacy. Gentler ways would be better.

Mary Kayitesi Blewitt

There are so many tasks that we women are doing to make the world a better place. If we could go to the top, it would be even better, because we would make the decisions. Women, more than men, can have real influence in stopping wars. I think for me it's more of a feminine thing, because we carry the babies. If you hear somebody else's child in the supermarket calling "Mum", it could be another person's child, but I always think they're calling me. My kids are grown, but that word "Mum" triggers a reaction, and you feel responsible, even though that child isn't yours. I do that and I think every woman does that. I turn around to see why they are calling.

Carla Del Ponte

If you give life, as women do when they have a child, it's more difficult to accept destroying life. But in history, we see also that women can be very cruel, so we must not generalize. To make a real difference, we need more women in positions of power.

> "Both sexes should try to be instrumental in stopping war."
>
> DAGMAR HAVLOVÁ

Christiane Amanpour

As a cautionary note, Condoleezza Rice is a woman, Margaret Thatcher was a woman, Catherine the Great was a woman – they all supported and went to war. But there are many women in this world who are working to stop wars and to make a difference in the world. They need to reach leadership positions in great numbers and not think that they have to act like men. I would also add the legions of women who I meet in my work and who, each and every one of them, are trying to make a difference and trying to resist the injustices and traditional prejudices against women.

Wangari Maathai

Women can make a difference, just as men can. I think that it's very important that we give women an opportunity to participate in power-sharing so we can see how they would behave once given that power. Sometimes I think we romanticize women and say that they would be more compassionate if they had power, but I don't necessarily believe that. We need to change the system and the values it has given rise to. Many women reach power by going along with the current system, so it's hard for them to break out of that masculine mould.

> “We need to recognize that women are already holding high office in many countries, and are involved in positions that can bring about a different vision.”
>
> MARY ROBINSON

Mary Robinson

I believe that we need to recognize that women are already holding high office in many countries, and are involved in positions that can bring about a different vision. It's important that the 21st century becomes a century of equal participation by women at all levels. I was involved in a Women Leaders Intercultural Forum, which looked at how women could provide leadership on human security issues. We brought together a number of women, former heads of state and government and international voices, to create a new vision of human security. One aim was to stop the terrible trade in small arms, which become the weapons of mass destruction. Another was to focus precisely on the main issues of our time, from nuclear proliferation, to our failure to deal with situations like Darfur.

Maya Angelou

I don't really allow differences between women and men. There was someone called the "Bitch of Buchenwald" who boasted that she had made a lampshade of people's skin. And the Ku Klux Klan wore sheets that women had made for them. So I don't impugn men more than women. As a group, I think that women have sometimes been more cowardly than men. We don't admit it, but we submit to what they want, and sometimes we know better but we agree to have our morals compromised.

Hanan Ashrawi

Yes, I feel I have a responsibility to make a difference both as a woman and as a human being. As a woman, I have larger handicaps and obstacles, but that just motivates me more. As a woman who has known first hand what it means to be on the receiving end of conflict, war, violence, injustice and discrimination, I believe I must not only stand up against these things but also make sure that they are faced collectively, not just individually. I certainly believe that wars are man-made rather than woman-made. But supportive and gender-sensitive people of either sex have a responsibility to stop wars and oppose violence and rampaging power, because we are on the receiving end in our daily lives, not just at a national and more dramatic level.

“I don’t really allow differences between women and men.”

MAYA ANGELOU

Kim Phuc

Women can make a difference with hope, love and forgiveness. I think women are more powerful than men. They know what real love is, and they need it, because women and children suffer the most.

WHAT SPIRITUAL OR RELIGIOUS BELIEFS DO YOU HOLD? | 8

Louise Ridley

I'm not religious but I believe in trying to be kind at every opportunity you can, without expecting anything back.

Jane Fonda

I'm a feminist Christian. I was raised an atheist, and what changed my thinking, when I was 51, was the collapse of my second marriage. I think extreme pain, emotional, psychic, spiritual pain can crack you open, and after that happened to me, tendrils of reverence began to grow, which took me by surprise. I didn't understand it, I didn't expect it, I just kind of went with it. Then my third husband Ted Turner brought me to Georgia, and suddenly for the first time in my life, I felt myself surrounded by people of faith, and they weren't dummies. Jimmy and Rosalind Carter, and Andrew Young, and others. I would question them, and I began to study the Bible, and I became a Christian.

I enrolled in the Interdenominational Theological Center in Atlanta, which is the largest training centre for African-American ministers. I was the only white student. I studied the interpretation work of feminist women and systemic theology, and I began to read Elaine Pagels. The more I studied, the more I realized that the Christianity that I had been attracted to was betrayed back in the 4th century. I felt that Jesus was speaking about the things that I believe in most strongly. I think that at a certain point in

"Extreme pain, emotional, psychic, spiritual pain can crack you open, and after that happened to me, tendrils of reverence began to grow."

JANE FONDA

history before Jesus was born there was a reverence for the feminine spirit, and for the power of a woman, and that many people viewed God as neither masculine or feminine but dualistic. That was smashed with the development of the formal Church. But if you go to some of the writings or sayings of Jesus that didn't make it into the canons, what he is saying is that the masculine and the feminine have to be brought together in order for us to really be whole people. That, in a very awkward, primitive way, is what I want to try to help happen in the world, and it has to happen when kids are growing up, which is why I work with young people all the time. We have to raise girls to claim their power and we have to raise boys to re-claim their hearts that get messed up at about five years old. Interestingly enough, I realize now that in the last third of life, women can come back to the strength and assertiveness they had before adolescence, and men can become more nurturing, sensitive and empathetic people, like they were when they were very young.

Isabel Allende

I am not a religious person but I have created a spiritual practice, which includes meditation. My commandments are very simple: do not harm anybody or anything, and whenever possible, do good.

Maya Angelou

I'm trying to be a Christian. I'm working at it, and it's no small matter. I'm always amazed when people come up to me and say: "I'm a Christian." I always think, oh really?! Trying to be a Christian is like trying to be a Muslim or a Jew or a Shintoist or Taoist. It's not thinking you're going to become one. It's putting yourself on the path.

Swanee Hunt

I love the metaphor of the King being born in the barn, and social order being turned on its head. So I adopt the idea of the crucified God, which is identification of God with suffering and with universal love.

"Trying to be a Christian is like trying to be a Muslim or a Jew or a Shintoist or Taoist. It's not thinking you're going to become one. It's putting yourself on the path."

MAYA ANGELOU

Benazir Bhutto

I am a Muslim and I believe in the Day of Judgment. Actually Muslim means those who believe, who submit before the will of one God. So in fact the term Muslim used to cover members of the Christian and Judean faiths because they also believe in a monolithic God. Then we were called "Mohammedans" during British rule to separate us as the followers of Mohammed. I believe in Islam, and I believe that all the great religions teach something in common, which is to do good in this world because we are judged on what we do here. And that all religions find common ground in setting out what is right and what is wrong.

I've often thought I would like to teach young people because they seem to be veering away from the real message of Islam. All these middle-class students are turning towards an extreme form of our religion, but this is happening because the books are written that way and there's nobody to tell them what the real message is. I remember I used to read books that told you heaven would be filled with young boys, and I used to question that, because I couldn't believe that God would fill heaven only with young boys. When I read the Koran itself, and went into the root-word that was used, it was not "boys" but "youth" – meaning that we will all be youthful in heaven.

Mary Robinson

I have a strong sense of spirituality, grounded in my Catholic upbringing. That's been broadened by marrying a Protestant and knowing that there was much about Catholic Ireland that had to be opened up. I was in Geneva some time ago with a very close friend of mine from Kenya. I went to a Lutheran two-hour service one Sunday, and found it wonderfully spiritually uplifting because it was so multicultural. I respect all religions in the role that they can play in reinforcing the dignity and worth of every individual. I recognize the downside that wars are being fought in the name of religion, so we have to ensure that faith leaders understand their responsibilities and, in particular, take responsibility for supporting gender equality. At the moment they are not sufficiently committed to that.

Mairead Maguire

I come from a Catholic background and believe very much that my faith has strengthened me. I always ask myself what Jesus would do, he's an important model in my life.

There are many paths to God and God lives in the hearts of all men and women, whether or not they're believers. We are interconnected as the human family. We need each other.

Jody Williams

I'm a spiritual vagabond, and totally atheist. I believe in a life force, but that sounds like *Star Trek*. I believe in an energy. I don't know if it motivates, but there is something there. It's certainly not the institutional benevolent God, I think that's bullshit. There's no way I could see a benevolent God allowing what goes on in the world.

Joan Baez

I practise Vipassana, a Buddhist meditation in which you sit down and try to be present – try to be aware of what is going on inside you, and just outside you, and in the world. You try to be quiet and watch your brain race around, which it does, and once a week or so mine is quiet for 45 seconds, and that is a very big deal for me. It is difficult, and in a way awful, because it shows that your mind really has control over you, and so it is a process of trying to get at least a look at what is going on. A lot of catastrophic thought! You could say that meditation is trying to make friends with your brain.

> “God lives in the hearts of all men and women, whether or not they're believers. We are interconnected as the human family.”
>
> MAIREAD MAGUIRE

Tanni Grey-Thompson

I'm not an atheist but I'm kind of agnostic. I believe there is something out there, but I'm just not quite sure what it is. Religious stuff and church services don't do anything for me. In the film *Men in Black* there is a bit at the end where only aliens are alive on earth, the camera pulls back and you see the world, and then you see the universe, and then you see eons and eons and eons, and it turns out we're only one little marble in this alien's game. I just wonder if we're an experiment in an alien lab somewhere. There's so much that is completely and utterly unexplained, and so I believe there is some power out there, something else.

Yoko Ono

Spirit lives. Religion kills.

Helen Prejean

I'm a Christian who follows the radical Jesus, who works for change in the world with the oppressed and the despised. I'm not following what I call the domesticated Jesus, quoted in churches on Sunday, where hymns are sung about the mercy of God, and then people support the execution of human beings. The way of Jesus is the way of compassion, and love, and community that does justice without violence, and in that way brings peace.

Emma Bonino

I hold ideals rather than beliefs. Beliefs tend to become dogmas. And religious beliefs, in particular, have caused and are still causing too much suffering around the world. So my ideals are definitely of a secular sort: freedom, democracy, the rule of law.

Kate Clinton

In my family we actively followed the Catholic way of doing the beatitudes, visiting the sick and helping people. That practical aspect is what I take from the Catholic approach. My own spiritual leaning is towards the belief that God is the great outdoors. That the tide comes in and the tide goes out.

Wangari Maathai

My spiritual beliefs started off at a very traditional level, then I was introduced very early on into Christian ideas and since that time I have been exposed to a lot of broader, ecumenical beliefs. I guess I would call myself a very liberal Christian. I believe in God but not necessarily in any form of organized religion.

Mariane Pearl

I have been a Buddhist for many years.

"Spirit lives. Religion kills."

YOKO ONO

Soledad O'Brien

I'm Catholic. I believe that there is a God, and that there is a reason for things that happen in the world. I separate Church and State, so I think of myself as religious, but with some very strong ideas about what is fair in the world for everybody. I think that tolerance of all religions is really important.

Kathy Kelly

I am still very compelled by the gospel. I don't mean everything in the New Testament, but the core values. The Catholic Worker Movement is something I always find moving. I very much appreciate what's been done through the network of Houses of Hospitality.

Jung Chang

I was not brought up with religious beliefs, because under Mao all religions were banned. Do I believe in God? No, but I do believe in some human qualities which I think are important. I would rank justice and kindness very high, also true charity and a sense of decency. These are more important things in life than being a big achiever.

Christiane Amanpour

I am religious and I believe that it provides a crucial moral framework.

Mary Kayitesi Blewitt

I'm Catholic, but I'm not driven by that. I can just as easily go to a mosque and pray and feel that I'm part of what they're doing, as I can go to any other church. So, religion, for me, is more the sense of inner self and of being comfortable with everything that's around you.

Martha Lane Fox

I'm not religious, but I would term myself agnostic rather than atheistic. I believe in people, in the power of people to hold each other together. I think I'd want to base any kind of belief system on the ability of individuals to trust and rely on their own powers.

Shirin Ebadi

I am a Muslim, and I have raised my two daughters as Muslims. Spirituality plays a big role in my Islamic perspective. Believing in God makes you more powerful. When I'm caught in difficult circumstances, I start thinking about God, and that empowers me to overcome that situation.

> "Believing in God makes you more powerful. When I'm caught in difficult circumstances, I start thinking about God, and that empowers me to overcome that situation."
>
> SHIRIN EBADI

Hanan Ashrawi

I believe in human values and ethical standards that make human life worth living. Two of my aunts are Catholic nuns and another is a Quaker. One uncle is a Baptist and another is Greek Orthodox. My father is agnostic and humanist and my sister married a Muslim. We have everything in our family. We live a life that is tolerant, accepting and inclusive of others. To me, the important thing now is to be a good human being. Whether this comes from God, or upbringing or convictions and faith, I can't discuss.

Judi Dench

I'm a Quaker. I went to a Quaker boarding school and found that the way a Quaker meeting is formed just from a group of people sitting together was so perfect for me. People get up and say things, but sitting for an hour and not speaking is a mind discipline which I need because I'm a flitter-abouter.

Bianca Jagger

I went to a Catholic convent and I remain a Catholic. I think that working on the death penalty issue and with people on Death Row has made me even closer to God than I was before.

Dagmar Havlová

I am a Christian, but I am very tolerant of other religions. Buddhism is very close to me and the charisma of the Dalai Lama affects me greatly. I put faith in my conscience, which tells me that I am doing something right or something wrong. And I turn to God when I feel worst, not only when searching my conscience, but in my desire for hope.

Sinéad O'Connor

I'm Catholic by birth and by culture, but I don't consider myself to belong to any particular religion. I'm inspired by all of them in some ways. God and religion are two different things, so I'm into God and I'm interested in religions but not stupid enough to belong to any one of them.

> "The way a Quaker meeting is formed just from a group of people sitting together was so perfect for me."
>
> JUDI DENCH

Shami Chakrabarti

I tend not to talk about this stuff because I have a public position and a job to do. I try and concentrate on what I'm confident about. And what I'm very certain about is the idea of human dignity and the idea that the individual cannot just be sacrificed to the greater good. I'm less confident about the sources, the ultimate sources of that certainty. But I believe the idea of human dignity and worth to be universal and common to all the great world religions at their best, rather than at their worst.

Mary McAleese

I'm a very simple follower of Christ, and of the gospel of love that attracted me to Him. Within the discipline of the Christian Churches I am a member of the Roman Catholic denomination, born and baptized into it, and I have stayed with it through thick and thin despite ups and downs and occasional misgivings. I don't agree with absolutely everything, but it is my spiritual home.

Marie Colvin

I was raised as a Catholic. I don't follow the rules and regulations of organized religion. But I do believe in God. I believe that there is something larger than we are, that we are not just pieces of meat. And as somebody once said, there are no atheists in the trenches.

Carla Del Ponte

I grew up in the Catholic Christian religion and I am still there, but I am not a practising Catholic. I have sometimes been upset with God because He allowed things to happen that I disagreed with totally. But I do believe in God.

Nataša Kandić

I don't believe in God. I believe in truth, I believe in human beings, I believe in justice.

Kim Phuc

In my teens, I was a devout follower of the Cao Đài religion, in my village Tây Ninh. I was looking for something to help me spiritually. I now believe in Jesus Christ. That has helped me. The Christian faith has helped me.

Tracey Emin

I believe that when we die we become light. I believe that every single thing is connected, every event, every moment. I couldn't live without believing, I would crumble. I believe in another dimension, another place.

> "There are no atheists in the trenches."
>
> MARIE COLVIN

DO YOU HAVE ANY ADVICE FOR THE YOUNGER GENERATION? | 9

Joan Baez

I think the younger generation needs to be listened to, because the young are not going to listen to advice. I certainly didn't. I think when the kids get a little bit older, well maybe much older – my son is 48 – they suddenly become respectable elders. For a while, the only elder my son respected was black and was playing a drum, and was just holy ground and light, someone you put beads on. And a mother could get slammed in a doorway in the stampede to see that elder. Now it's fine, but I had to voice what I felt! Once when my mother came in the room – she was 93, and the kids were all sitting around, nobody stood up – mother said, "Oh, don't get up, anyone!" in a sarcastic way. I said, "You know you guys, get up and I'll explain it later." That is just what happened. You show respect by getting up. A very sweet niece of mine said, "Thank you for telling me. I had no idea." And she meant it. There seem to be better manners in Europe, it's a matter of training.

"I think the younger generation needs to be listened to, because the young are not going to listen to advice."

JOAN BAEZ

Severn Cullis-Suzuki

We need the younger generation to speak up to the older generation and tell them to take responsibility. Young people need to be the voice of truth. They're the ones who have the kind of credibility that can cut through to people who aren't used to thinking in terms of what kind of repercussions their actions have. There's nothing more powerful than a child asking their parents why there is injustice in the world and asking them what they're doing about it. We need their voice. People still talk about the speech I gave at the age of 12 at the UN Conference on Environment and Development in Rio de Janeiro in 1992. My hope with the Rio speech was that young people would follow that example or hear me speaking and realize, "Hey, I can speak up too."

Soledad O'Brien

I think it was Gandhi who said, "Be the change you want to see." There is something very true about that.

> "There's nothing more powerful than a child asking their parents why there is injustice in the world and asking them what they're doing about it."
>
> SEVERN CULLIS-SUZUKI

Helen Prejean

What I say to young people is, ignite, get passionate about something you really believe in. Don't spend your lives on these trivial agendas where you work to make rich people richer, or just to accumulate material possessions. You want a soul-sized agenda for your life. Yes, it will make you tired, and yes, it will break your heart, but you are going to be part of the wave of the future and helping love and compassion to be real in the world. Feel the energy of life come through you. You may be defeated in some of the tasks that you try to accomplish on behalf of people who have no one else to defend them, but you will never be so alive. The Lebanese poet Khalil Gibran once said that you should do a life's work that causes you to laugh all your laughter and cry all your tears.

Shami Chakrabarti

I'll tell you what I want for my son. I want him to believe that he's anybody's equal, but at the same time, that he's no one's superior. That's quite a difficult trick to pull off. To be confident, and proud of yourself and your beliefs, but at the same time not to be arrogant, or smug, or superior, is something that we all struggle with. A lot of people – women particularly – are kind, generous and altruistic, but are self-deprecating to the point of not valuing themselves. On the other hand, some very successful, very creative, very inspiring people are confident and proud, and show leadership skills and all the rest of it, but lack humility. And when you lack humility, all sorts of devastating consequences follow, particularly if you have a lot of power. At the same time, I would say to young people that it helps to be happy with yourself. You have to love yourself a little bit in order to be a good friend and a good colleague, I really do think that these things are connected. Great big political causes for justice, and so on, can become far too abstract if you don't try and live the values in your personal life at home as well. If we try and live the values at home, as well as at work, we'll all be happier.

Maya Angelou

Try to convince yourself that you're not the only thing in the universe, or the best or the worst in the universe. It's very important to have an idea that there's something greater than you, so you can pull yourself away from your egomania.

> "I'll tell you what I want for my son. I want him to believe that he's anybody's equal, but at the same time, that he's no one's superior."
>
> SHAMI CHAKRABARTI

Kate Clinton

When I talk to younger people, I ask, "What are you interested in? What are you passionate about? Well, why not bring other people together, not through an email, not through a chat room, but actually to have dinner at your house, and talk about what you can do?" Real communication does not happen with an iPhone. In fact, the really wonderful kind of sexy excitement is actually doing things, political things, face to face with other people. We really can affect change.

Shirin Ebadi

I always tell young people to have self-confidence. Don't be scared of making mistakes. I think that one of the rights of a human being is the right to make mistakes. What counts is to learn lessons from them and not insist on continuing guiltily on a mistaken course.

Mary McAleese

Well, my children never listen to the advice that I give them, so I have no great expectations that any member of the younger generation is going to listen to anything I say, unless it's to believe emphatically in the power of one. To believe they are on this earth to do something wonderful for themselves and for others. And to believe in their ability to do it no matter what obstacles and no matter what self-doubt lurks. As simple as that.

Judi Dench

I expect young people have lots of advice for me. I don't even have an answering machine! What concerns me is young people who don't see their parents because they don't understand them, and say their parents don't understand them. Where on earth do you go from there? My husband Michael and I bought a house where his parents and my ma, and all of us, lived together. We ate together, we did everything together. We just had a bedroom and a bathroom, and shared everything else. Finty, my daughter, remembers it as a wonderful time with her grandparents around her all the time.

Kathy Kelly

I'd say that there is no gift greater in life than the privilege of being able to live in harmony with your deepest values. You have to focus, because you can't solve every problem. And it's okay to start somewhere even if you haven't "lined up all your ducks", because if you wait until you're perfect, you'll wait a very long time.

Sinéad O'Connor

What I tell my children is that grown-ups are all stupid, so it's down to them. I think they know better than we do. But if I needed to say one thing to kids, I'd say don't do chemical drugs.

Jody Williams

Get up off your ass and do something. Find a number of organizations and volunteer an hour a month, until you find one that you feel comfortable with. Give up an hour at Starbucks having a latte, or give up an hour at the mall shopping. Go do something good with your time. One hour a month. If everybody did that, imagine the world. If you care about something, go do something about it or shut up and let those of us who want to do something about it get on with it.

Marie Colvin

Follow your heart, find something you really care about. Don't ever let anyone or anything convince you that you can't do what you believe you can. For journalists covering wars – and I lost an eye in one – I would say that you have to look clearly at the issues and not say, "Soldier equals bad," and "Person who won't shoot someone equals good." I think force is something that is often resorted to far too easily and too quickly, but sometimes it's necessary. Soldiers often fight wars that they don't want to. In World War II, they believed they were fighting evil. I do believe that if there is evil you have to fight it. If that means picking up a gun, then yes, I would do that. I'm a non-pacifist. I would fight for my family, I would fight for what I believed in, and I would do it with a gun if I had to.

> “Go do something good with your time. One hour a month. If everybody did that, imagine the world.”
>
> JODY WILLIAMS

Paloma Picasso

Young people should believe that they can make a difference, and that we are really going to have to make an effort at living together better if we don't want this world to explode and end in misery. I'm afraid at this point that this is what we are seeing with people fighting each other about their different faiths, or behaving violently because they are getting lost in the world and don't know where they belong. They are looking at their religion or country as something to identify with, something to differentiate themselves from the others, instead of trying to adopt a unifying love. I grew up in the '60s, so we all hoped that the world was going to become one and that there would no longer be any frontiers ... you know, love and peace. That's what we were marching for, and still many years down the line, it just hasn't happened. TV has made us all much more aware of the misery and disasters happening all over the world. But if young people don't have a belief that things can be better, and the desire to try and improve them, then there is no hope.

Jane Fonda

I work with adolescent boys and girls, and all the work aims towards saying to the boys that being a man has nothing to do with knocking up a lot of girls and having babies that you don't take care of, and trying to be macho. And saying to girls you have the right to be who you are, to protect yourself, and to have agency over your body, and to really know what you want and what you don't want, and to say it loudly and clearly. I wrote a book for boys and girls, and again it's the gender distortions that I was trying to unravel. The idea that a woman is "property" and that a man always has to prove his superiority has been around so long that we think it's wallpaper. But it's not inevitable, and I think it's going to be women and men of conscience who change that social attitude, just as it is they who are beginning to change our present attitude to the environment.

Louise Ridley

Know that if you don't take the initiative to make something happen, it probably won't. Be your own champion and a champion for people who could do with your support too.

Nataša Kandić

I think that it is important for the coming generation to know about and to learn from the past. Without that, nothing will improve.

Carla Del Ponte

My advice to the young generation is be very single-minded about the absolute importance of peace, peace at every level. They should strive for peace in the family, in relationships with friends, in social life and of course in politics. That is my strong message, because for eight years as UN Prosecutor I saw how much suffering is caused to the victims of crimes against humanity, and crimes committed during armed conflict.

Mary Robinson

As a mother and grandmother, I know that the best advice is not what you say but what you do. I enjoy the company of young people; I've been teaching all my life and still teach very bright students at Columbia University. I like to learn from the young as much as teach them. Our Women Leaders Intercultural Forum was intercultural, interregional and, very importantly, intergenerational. We were trying to link with young women and get a sense of what leadership meant to them and what the issues were. Their perspective was different, and it was good to learn together. Teaching by example is the best way.

Isabel Allende

Be connected, talk to each other, share ideas, take care of the planet and of each other, and be joyful.

> "Be connected, talk to each other, share ideas, take care of the planet and of each other, and be joyful."
>
> ISABEL ALLENDE

Wangari Maathai

It's always tempting to tell people how they should live and what they should do. I think that for the younger generation the main thing is to tell them to maintain their hope, not to give up, and to take care of their health. So many of them face temptations to destroy their health in one way or another that I feel it's very important for them to realize how crucial it is to take care of themselves.

Tanni Grey-Thompson

I think you should have a belief that you can challenge the status quo. It's not about material things. It's not about whether you have the latest mobile phone or any of that kind of fluff. You have to do something with your life rather than being famous for being famous. Some young people seem to believe that a pop star's hairstyle is more important than what's happening in Afghanistan. I guess my message would be to do something properly.

Bianca Jagger

I always say to young people that they must realize that they can make a difference in the world and must become engaged and try to influence politicians. If each person became conscious of the power of the individual, we would live in a completely different world.

Dagmar Havlová

I would advise young people not to repeat the mistakes of the older generation, or repeat their own mistakes either, because a person only has the right to repeat a mistake once. To be suitably humble but not afraid of obstacles. To want to educate themselves and work on improving everything possible in society. And to empathize with the needs of others. Social feeling is diminishing in all countries.

Kim Phuc

As a Goodwill Ambassador for UNESCO, working for peace, I think young people should try to help children of war, who need a voice, who need help from other people around the world. I was that little girl in Vietnam, in the wrong place at the wrong time. I am now in the right place at the right time, but I will never forget where I came from. Learn how to live with true love.

> “You have to stand up for what you believe is right, and you can’t accept imposed definitions of your own value or worth. Define your own value and worth.”
>
> HANAN ASHRAWI

Mary Kayitesi Blewitt

Young people shouldn’t settle for simply being bystanders. We adults should be doing more to train our children to stand up for what’s right. If someone is being bullied, or if you know instinctively that something isn’t right, you should act, and not walk away from the situation.

Hanan Ashrawi

My advice is the same advice I was given when I was young. Have confidence, because you’re not alone: there are others who will support you. Secondly, don’t let yourself be intimidated. You have to stand up for what you believe is right, and you can’t accept imposed definitions of your own value or worth. Define your own value and worth, and have confidence in yourself as a human being.

Mairead Maguire

I'd say work on your inner peace. Take time to find that inner peace and to deal with the conflict that's going on inside yourself. I think the greatest wars are really inside our own minds, our own hearts, dealing with our emotions, because we're so human and life is very hard, and it's not easy for anybody. Believe in yourself, and believe that you are loved by God and loved by many people, and love yourself. I would like to appeal to young people who might get involved in suicide bombings to remember that all life is sacred. Bombs are not the way to solve our problems.

Marion Cotillard

I think we should listen to the younger generation. They are smart and aware of what is happening. They are begging us to have more respect for what we are going to leave them. My advice to them would be to help or force the old generation to wake up!

Yoko Ono

Do what you can for the health of the planet. But don't forget to also have fun.

Paula Rego

Work hard. Find something you want to do and work at it. Get better at it and have a good time. I see my children and grandchildren and they all seem to be okay. I have no advice for them at all.

Martha Lane Fox

My advice would be to push yourself, to believe you can do things even if they seem a bit scary or daunting, and to believe that they will go right. There's no doubt I'd still be in hospital, possibly even in a wheelchair, if I wasn't an optimistic person and hadn't fought back after my accident and stubbornly believed that I could walk again. Equally, I believe at a professional level that businesses are more likely to be successful when you're being confident and exuding positivism.

> "It's important to get beyond the 'me', to think of your family, your community and what you can give back to your community. I don't just mean financially – it can be a kind word or a shoulder to cry on."
>
> BENAZIR BHUTTO

Benazir Bhutto

I want to tell the younger generation that in the desire to succeed and get ahead, it's very important not to lose contact with one's own family, because I think that the sense of community feeling is born from within the family. I think that it's also important to try and make a marriage work and that people should make an effort in a marriage to keep it together. So while I'm not against divorce, which can be very important in certain circumstances, I would tell young people to make more of an effort to compromise. Not just in marital relations, but generally. Sometimes I feel that this is too much the "me" generation. It's important to get beyond the "me", to think of your family, your community and what you can give back to your community. I don't just mean financially – it can be a kind word or a shoulder to cry on. These small things can be a great support system. There is more to life than just success, because you can be very successful and end up being lonely. Financial wealth and material comfort are one sort of richness, but emotional support and community feeling is another kind of wealth – a lot more powerful.

Jung Chang

I would say to young people that being a good person comes before everything else, and it is not incompatible with being a good professional, or writer, or statesman. It is important to be a good human being first.

Swanee Hunt

I'd encourage young people to be active in confronting the problems that they see around them. Our society leads them to think that life is about acquiring things. But the deepest fulfilment is to know that you're part of shaping the world.

Christiane Amanpour

I think that young people should have a dream and a passion, that they should work hard, and that they should believe in their power to change the world for the better. They should not just be empty fame junkies.

DO YOU HAVE A FAVOURITE WORK OF ART, BOOK, POEM OR PIECE OF MUSIC THAT HAS A SPECIAL PERSONAL SIGNIFICANCE FOR YOU? | 10

Mary McAleese

I have always loved the old Irish poem by James Clarence Mangan called "Roísín Dubh", which translates as "My Dark Rosaleen". The resonance of it has never left me. It's about this beautiful, strong woman who at every turn and twist of her life is thwarted in the realization of her full freedom, her full dignity, her full equality. She is a metaphor for Ireland. The poem became one of the most famous of all Irish songs and was later used by Séan Ó Riada, a wonderful composer, as part of the musical score for a film called *Mise Eire*, which means very simply "I am Ireland". It was released in 1960, and I went to see it when I was nine years old. It's about the War of Independence, and is incredibly passionate. The music is so stirring that it has never left me, because it summarized the place I was in the world, the place where I could make a difference. At the time, 1960s Ireland was a very bleak place, but here was this powerful, brilliant music, and it was music I was familiar with, but now it had been given a new dimension and a new spirit.

I heard "My Dark Rosaleen" first in my own home where my aunt could play it on the piano and sing it. She was a woman with a lot to lament and a future yet to be realized, and I am so lucky and so privileged to be part of a generation now that has allowed Dark Rosaleen to shine, to show her face to the world, to be a member of the European Union. For me the song is all about destiny. This generation is very,

very close to having the equality, the peace, the freedom from sectarianism, the reconciliation and joy that so many people in Ireland never, ever had.

Jung Chang

One of my favourite artistic possessions is an 18th-century dish that my grandmother hid with great ingenuity during the Cultural Revolution when antiques in people's homes were being smashed as part of the "anti-bourgeois" hysteria. That dish is to me a kind of a symbol of the precariousness of Chinese culture, which suffered so many traumas under Mao and is still suffering today. When I was a teenager, exiled to the Himalayas and very ill, I read a novella, *First Love* by Turgenev, that was very close to my heart, and doubly precious because it was a smuggled copy my entrepreneurial young brother had bought on the black market. In those days, all music was banned except for songs in praise of Mao. The lyrics were extremely limited but, strangely, some of the tunes were very beautiful.

Christiane Amanpour

I have two favourite poems. One is Kipling's "If". The other is "The Village Blacksmith" by Longfellow. Among many, many books are *Pride and Prejudice*, *Jane Eyre* and *The Kite Runner*. And I love Handel's *Water Music*.

Maya Angelou

I collect art, and a major piece in my collection is a magnificent picture by the African-American artist John Biggers who painted it while he was in Ghana. When I was a guest on the BBC programme *Desert Island Discs* I chose his picture as one thing I would like to have with me if I was stranded. I also chose a book called *The Negro Caravan*, a collection of writing by African-Americans with excerpts from slaves in the 19th century, poetry dating back to the 18th century and other writing up to 1940 when the book was published. It was pulled together by three poets, and some of it is so beautiful that just thinking about it makes you weep that it exists.

There's a 19th-century African-American poet, Ann Spencer, who wrote "Letter to my Sister", which inspired me to write my book. The poem says: "It is dangerous for a woman/ To defy the gods;/ To taunt them with the tongue's thin tip,/ Or strut in the weakness/ Of mere humanity,/ Or draw a line daring them to cross;/ The gods own the searing lightning,/ The drowning waters, tormenting fears/ And anger of red sins."

I'm partial to American music, jazz, blues, country and gospel. I do like some of the European classics but am closest to the operas of Puccini and Verdi. I like the Russian composers too, big and huge, like their land.

> "I chose a book called *The Negro Caravan*, a collection of writing by African-Americans ... some of it is so beautiful that just thinking about it makes you weep that it exists."
>
> MAYA ANGELOU

Kathy Kelly

I love the poetry of Wilfred Owen, who was killed in France in the last week of World War I. I wish that somehow we could tap him on the shoulder and say: "Hey, guess what? Your words have travelled across borders and over decades." I'm deeply moved by his youthful desire to communicate on behalf of those others who were dying close to him. Another who has moved me by the honesty and skill of his writing is Primo Levi, who survived the Auschwitz concentration camp. I'm grateful for classical music. Leonard Cohen also has a great deal of meaning for me.

> "I'm deeply moved by Wilfred Owen's youthful desire to communicate on behalf of those others who were dying close to him."

>
> KATHY KELLY

> "I like *The Scream* by Edvard Munch ... It just makes me laugh every time I see it."
>
> SINÉAD O'CONNOR

Bianca Jagger

Gandhi's book *Non-Violent Resistance* was a great influence on me. In art I love Matisse, Picasso (especially in his Blue Period) and Andy Warhol. Also the British sculptor Antony Gormley, famous for his *Angel of the North*. Music that I love is Wagner's *Tristan and Isolde*, Verdi's *Requiem*, the Buena Vista Social Club, and Bob Dylan singing "Blowin' in the Wind".

Sinéad O'Connor

The most inspiring book I've ever read is the *Tankah*, basically the Jewish equivalent of our Old Testament, except that we stole it from them so it's the original. It's the thing I would grab if the house caught fire. My favourite music is Gregorian chants. There's a group of monks in Ireland from a place called Glenstal Abbey who made a couple of records of just Gregorian chants, and I like that best. In painting, I like *The Scream* by Edvard Munch. I think it's very funny as well, but nobody else seems to think it's funny. It just makes me laugh every time I see it.

Helen Prejean

I love Handel's *Messiah*, and the part, "Oh look and see if there is any sorrow greater to my sorrow", because I have tasted so much of that when I've been with people who have been executed. I think the music that Tim Robbins did with the Pakistani singer Nusrat Fateh Ali Khan was beautiful in the film *Dead Man Walking*. It's the kind of singing that must be passed on from family to family. And I love the Beatles, the energy of their music. In art, I generally like strong painters like Georges Rouault. There's a strength to the paintings of Edward Hopper that I like. A book that changed my life is *Jesus Before Christianity* by Albert Nolan, about how Jesus took on the temple cult of his day as well as the Roman authorities because he was standing with the marginalized and oppressed. I have been living out of it ever since.

Swanee Hunt

Gustav Mahler's "Adagietto" from his Fifth Symphony is such a beautiful piece of music that I cry every time I hear it. And I have a favourite poem by Thomas Hardy called "The Oxen" written during World War I – it's about the preservation of faith, no matter what the circumstance. We have a portrait of Nureyev by the American painter Jamie Wyeth that is a particular love of mine. It encapsulates such beauty and grace in the human body, even though you don't see him moving, but just his beautiful ballet stance.

Ann Leslie

I couldn't live without Shakespeare and I love poetry: Keats, Larkin and Neruda especially. When I'm tired or depressed I re-read novels I already know backwards, mostly Jane Austen and Thomas Hardy. I'm like a child who wants to listen to the same favourite story over and over again, like a comfort blanket. I'm not very musical – a great sadness for my husband who constantly tried to "educate" me by dragging me off to string quartet recitals and opera. Poor lamb, he's given up now. Music that really moves me tends to be Indian classical music, perhaps because of my childhood in India.

Judi Dench

I'll choose the whole of Shakespeare. Oh, and hundreds of paintings. There is a wonderful painting by Patrick Caulfield of a great jug, which I absolutely adore, and another favourite is the *Primavera* by Botticelli.

> "I re-read novels I already know backwards ... I'm like a child who wants to listen to the same favourite story over and over again."
>
> ANN LESLIE

> “I get nostalgic when Frank Sinatra sings ‘Strangers in the Night’ because my father used to play it, and it was playing when he met my mother.”
>
> BENAZIR BHUTTO

Benazir Bhutto

I love art. I don’t buy famous pictures though, but simple paintings that speak to my heart. One that I bought from Hyde Park Corner was so cheerful, it just invited me to be cheerful and happy, and made me feel that life was full of perfumes and colours and the gifts of nature. Each painting that I have tells a story. None is expensive, but they are very precious to me. When I was at university I loved listening to pop songs. My father liked classical music very much, and he used to tell me that I listened to rubbish when I was playing Roberta Flack or Diana Ross. I’m still nostalgic for the 1970s when I hear Diana Ross singing “Touch Me in the Morning”. I also get nostalgic when Frank Sinatra sings “Strangers in the Night”, because my father used to play it, and it was playing when he met my mother. I bought it for her because she has got Alzheimer’s and I thought she might like to hear it.

Joan Baez

I have a favourite singer, Jussi Björling, the Swedish opera singer. To me, he is the finest tenor who ever lived. He died at the age of 49 in 1960. He was a terrible actor but had the most exquisite voice, transcendent when he did his own recitals. When you ask me about art, what I see in my head is the anonymous Greek sculpture *La Victoire*, called "Winged Victory" in English. It stands at one end of the Louvre, and sort of rises off the big pedestal it is on. It's just beautiful.

Tanni Grey-Thompson

I have some favourite words, very emotional ones, that my mum liked and wrote down, and which we found among her things when she died: "Death is nothing at all. It does not count. I have only slipped away into the next room. Nothing has happened. Everything remains exactly as it was. I am I and you are you, and the old life we lived so fondly together is untouched, unchanged …"

Dagmar Havlová

I would probably start my list of favourites with the Dalai Lama's book *The Art of Living and Dying* or *An Open Heart*. I like Kundera's *Immortality*, and also the plays of my husband, Václav Havel, because they contain humour. I love visiting art museums, because I find security and certainty there. The painters I like most are Van Gogh, Lautrec and Monet.

In music, I like a number of Moravian folk songs. They are especially wistful and come straight from the heart. The works of Tchaikovsky, Vivaldi and many other composers of classical music give me a sense of safety in a special way.

Tracey Emin

My favourite poem is an 11th-century Arabic poem by Ahmad Ibu-al-Qaf. If I could have a painting hanging in my house, it would be Vermeer's painting *The Love Letter*. If I could have a book to take with me somewhere it would be Spinoza's *Ethics*. I listen to all kinds of music – Leonard Cohen, Johnny Cash, David Bowie – but it's got to move me, and I have to really like the lyrics as well.

Mairead Maguire

I do love the book *The Imitation of Christ* by Thomas à Kempis, and the Bible. I love music, any piano pieces, such as Chopin. I love the piano and often think of Aung San Suu Kyi in Burma. She plays the piano, and it must have given her comfort and solace in her loneliness and confinement, so cut off from everyone.

> “I love visiting art museums ... I find security and certainty there.”
>
> DAGMAR HAVLOVÁ

Mary Robinson

Poetry has always had a special significance for me but I don't have a favourite. I have a bookshelf of poetry that I go to quite frequently, and I use the words of poets quite a lot in my own work. They say it so much better. Also, as a spiritual kind of reinforcement, I find that dipping into both familiar and less familiar works of poetry is a great solace, an enormous help. It's been a great blessing that my husband and his family have always enjoyed works of art. My daughter studied History of Art, so we have lots of books and many paintings that I'm very fond of, but I couldn't single out just one.

Martha Lane Fox

A favourite book for me would be *War and Peace*. It throws the most incredible shaft of light on different aspects of humanity and the human life cycle, and I always read it and feel both humbled and inspired at the same time. In art, I think that Vermeer is just completely extraordinary.

Jody Williams

If anybody asked what book I'd take to a desert island, I'd say the biggest dictionary in the world because you would never get tired of trying to learn all the words, and of what you could do with them. I love art, a lot of it Asian influenced – Chinese and Japanese. I also like music of my time – the Beatles.

> “*War and Peace* throws the most incredible shaft of light on different aspects of humanity and the human life cycle.”
>
> MARTHA LANE FOX

Emma Bonino

Khaled Hosseini's book *The Kite Runner* has a strong personal significance for me because it's about Afghanistan, a country that has a very special place in my heart.

Shirin Ebadi

I like reading the Indian writer Jhumpa Lahiri, who wrote the book on which the movie *The Namesake* was based, and also the work of Mira Nair who directed it. I try to read literature for half an hour every night. Persian literature mostly, because I speak, read and write Persian. But I also like reading books that have been translated into Persian. And I enjoy all kinds of music and art.

Marion Cotillard

First would be Harold Pinter's 2005 Nobel Prize acceptance speech, "Art, Truth and Politics". A book that has touched my soul is Jeremy Narby's *The Cosmic Serpent.*

Louise Ridley

I have a wonderful friend called Olivia who has far better and far wider music taste than me and has basically chosen a lot of my favourite music for me since we were at school together. One song is "Love and Affection" by Joan Armatrading. It reminds me of discovering music by swapping mini discs, and the music builds up gradually in the most powerful, understated way. "Tiny Dancer" by Elton John has always held a weird teenage nostalgia for me – after hearing it in the film *Almost Famous* in my teens, I suspect – and was the song my husband and I had as the first dance at our wedding. Poetry-wise, I'm about to have a baby and think "All The Things You Are Not Yet" by Helen Dunmore, and "Make the Ordinary Come Alive" by William Martin, sum up the wonder of creating a whole new person.

Kate Clinton

My favourite poems are by Muriel Rukeyser, a New York poet who began publishing in the 1930s and died in 1980. As well as being a poet, she was an activist and a war resister who wrote a very inspiring book called *The Life of Poetry*. I've just re-read it, and it really crystallizes my thoughts about the power people have to make a difference.

> “Fiction and film should provoke in that way.”
>
> SHAMI CHAKRABARTI

Paula Rego

I love Verdi, and listen to his *Rigoletto* nearly every Saturday morning. I like Puccini and Donizetti as well. I read a lot of poetry and look at painting all the time in order to learn. I'm a great admirer of William Berra, a very remarkable artist. I'm a great fan of Max Ernst, and I love Grünewald, who is extraordinary. I love all Spanish painting – Goya, of course, and Ribera. But I also like Italian painting – Caravaggio, Michelangelo. Picasso was a great master, a genius.

Shami Chakrabarti

I am slightly haunted by a film called *The Children of Men*. I think it's an excellent film and very thought provoking. Fiction and film should provoke in that way. Now I'm not trying to suggest that the apocalyptic scenario painted in that film is going to happen, that it's going to happen next year, or in a decade's time, or in a hundred years' time. But I think that some of the circumstances that make that kind of horrific outcome more likely are all too prevalent.

Hanan Ashrawi

I have many favourites in each area, depending on my mood. If I'm in a mood to indulge in the esoteric, I would say I like some old English literature. I like Chaucer, for example. Among poets, I love Mahmoud Darwish, a Palestinian poet. Also Yeats. I love reading, and like classical literature. I like Greek tragedy. I like books of criticism. And if I'm in the mood for politics, I love the books by Edward Said. I disagree with some of his views – we had a big argument over culture and imperialism – but still I think he's brilliant. I don't have exclusive favourites, but so many books, pieces of music, paintings and works of art have given depth, richness and variety to my life, and I appreciate all of them.

Mary Kayitesi Blewitt

Anything that makes my head move is nice. Anything that brings joy, however small it is, I absorb it. Music is actually very therapeutic for me. I like to listen to classical music. When I'm in the mood to dance, I dance to anything, hip-hop, anything. I'm a very, very simple person. I don't categorize things.

Marie Colvin

Yeats is my favourite poet. There's a line of his that I love, from a poem about the Easter Rising in Dublin: "A terrible beauty is born." Among artists, I admire a German painter called Anselm Kiefer who captures in an abstract way the extremes of humanity, and he can do it with just colour and bits and pieces. It's the kind of art that punches you in the stomach.

Nataša Kandić

I like Matisse's paintings. And I like listening to music and taking part in theatrical and musical activities.

Wangari Maathai

I love all kinds of music. When I was asked that question by the Norwegian Nobel Committee, I told them I wanted to hear the music of Patti LaBelle, an American singer who combines spirituals with soul music – quasi-spiritual, quasi-soul. I also enjoy classical music, especially hymns, classical hymns.

Soledad O'Brien

There's a wonderful Dominican artist called Rascal who works in New York City. I love his work because he always draws people and they are very colourful, so I have his artwork all over my house. In music, I think India.Arie is a terrific singer, also Melissa Etheridge.

Yoko Ono

Human civilization and culture are incredibly important to me. Let's not destroy the beauty we've created through centuries.

Kim Phuc

I love classical music. I love to draw. And I love the inspirational art of Thomas Kinkade. He is famous in North America, and I have one of his paintings in my house.

Isabel Allende

For inspiration, I read poetry, especially by Pablo Neruda.

Mariane Pearl

I have a favourite passage from a speech made by Robert F. Kennedy at the University of Cape Town on 6 June 1966 that begins, "Few will have the greatness to bend history, but each of us can work to change a small portion of events, and in the total of all those acts will be written the history of this generation."

Jane Fonda

Léger is one of my favourite artists. And my favourite poem is one of Rilke's *Sonnets to Orpheus* about the unicorn.

ABOUT THE CONTRIBUTORS

Isabel Allende

Novelist and activist. Allende's novels, including *The House of the Spirits, Eva Luna, Paula* and *Daughter of Fortune*, are international bestsellers. She is the founder of the Isabel Allende Foundation, working to empower and protect women worldwide. She received Chile's National Literature Prize in 2010 and was awarded the Presidential Medal of Freedom in 2014 by Barack Obama.

Christiane Amanpour, CBE

British-Iranian journalist and television host. Amanpour is the Chief International Anchor for CNN. She has reported from most of the major conflicts of the last two decades, including the Gulf War, the Bosnian War, Rwanda and Afghanistan. Amanpour has been the recipient of more than 60 awards, including 11 Emmys and four Peabody Awards. She was awarded a CBE in 2007.

Dr Maya Angelou

Poet, memoirist, playwright, civil rights activist, performer, stage and screen producer and director, songwriter and historian. She has been awarded over 50 honorary degrees and been nominated for major book and Grammy awards. She died in 2014, aged 86.

Dr Hanan Ashrawi

Legislator, human rights activist and scholar. She served as the official spokesperson for the Palestinian delegation to the Middle East peace process and is the founder of MIFTAH, the Palestinian Initiative for the Promotion of Global Dialogue and Democracy. Ashrawi was awarded the Sydney Peace Prize in 2003.

Joan Baez

Singer. Baez has been a human rights advocate and champion of non-violent resistance since she first became famous in the 1960s, linking her music with her actions on behalf of the civil rights and anti-war movements in the US. More recently she has been linked with the campaign for the abolition of the death penalty in the US and the anti-war effort concerning US policy in the Middle East. In 2011, Amnesty International held the inaugural event for the AI Joan Baez Award for Outstanding Inspirational Service in the Global Fight for Human Rights.

Benazir Bhutto

First female Prime Minister of Pakistan. Assassinated in 2007 shortly after this interview, Bhutto was then chairwoman of the Pakistan People's Party. She died two weeks before the scheduled Pakistani General Election, in which she would have been the leading opposition candidate to President Musharraf.

Mary Kayitesi Blewitt

Founder of the Survivors Fund for survivors of the Rwanda genocide (SURF). After losing 50 family members in the 1994 genocide, she volunteered for the Rwandan Ministry of Rehabilitation for eight months before setting up SURF. She received the Pilkington Award in 2004. She was awarded an OBE after running the Survivors Fund for 15 years.

Emma Bonino

Vice President of the Italian Senate, former European Commissioner and former Italian Minister of International Trade and European Affairs. She was awarded the North-South Prize in 1999 for her contribution toward human rights. She was Minister for Foreign Affairs 2013–14.

Shami Chakrabarti, Baroness Chakrabarti

Director of Liberty (National Council for Civil Liberties) from 2003 to 2016, which aims to protect civil liberties and promote human rights. She was Chancellor of Oxford Brookes University until 2015, and Chancellor of the University of Essex from 2014 to 2017. She was awarded a CBE in 2007.

Jung Chang

Writer. Her autobiographical account of three generations of Chinese women, *Wild Swans*, sold over 10 million copies worldwide. In 2005 she published *Mao: The Unknown Story*, with Jon Halliday, a historical account of Mao Zedong's life and work.

Kate Clinton

Political humorist and family entertainer. She has toured her national one-woman show many times, publishing nine comedy collections and four DVDs. She is the author of three books, *What the L?*, *Don't Get Me Started* and her third collection, *I Told You So.*

Marie Colvin

Foreign correspondent for the *Sunday Times* from 1985 till her death in 2012. Despite being seriously wounded in a Sri Lankan war zone, Colvin reported from nearly every violent conflict. She died while covering the siege of Homs in Syria.

Marion Cotillard

Actress. Cotillard won a César, a BAFTA and an Academy Award for Best Actress for her performance as Edith Piaf in *La Vie en Rose* (2007). She became a Knight of the Order of Arts and Letters in France in 2010 and promoted to Officer in 2016. She is the star of a number of movies, including *A Very Long Engagement*, *Innocence*, *Public Enemies*, *Inception* and *Rust and Bone*.

Severn Cullis-Suzuki

Environmental speaker, author and television host. She founded the Environmental Children's Organization in 1988, aged nine, and has continued to campaign for environmental causes, emphasizing personal responsibility in conservation.

Carla Del Ponte

Former Chief UN War Crimes Prosecutor. Del Ponte brought Slobodan Milošević to trial and prosecuted the Rwandan government for genocide, as well as war criminals and Mafia members. She is the author of the book *The Hunt: Me and the War Criminals*. She served as Swiss Ambassador to Argentina from 2008 to 2011.

Dame Judi Dench

Actress. She has received six Academy Award nominations, winning for her depiction of Queen Elizabeth in *Shakespeare in Love* (1998). Recipient of ten BAFTAs, two Golden Globes and a Tony, she has been a Dame Commander of the British Empire since 1988.

Dr Shirin Ebadi

Lawyer and human rights activist. She is founder of the Children's Rights Support Association in Iran, and the first Muslim woman to win the Nobel Peace Prize in 2003 for her contribution to human rights. She is the author of *Iran Awakening: A Memoir of Revolution and Hope*, *Refugee Rights in Iran*, *The Golden Cage* and *Until We Are Free.*

Tracey Emin, CBE

Artist. Emin was a Turner Prize nominee in 1999, represented Britain at the Venice Biennale and has been a Royal Academician since 2007. She has donated many works to charity auctions, and founded the Tracey Emin Library in Uganda in 2008. She was Professor of Drawing at the Royal Academy from 2011 to 2013. In 2013 she was awarded a CBE.

Jane Fonda

Actress and peace activist. Fonda starred in films such as *Barbarella*, *On Golden Pond* and *Nine to Five*, and has been a recipient of two Academy Awards. Since her opposition to the Vietnam War in the 1960s she has supported a variety of anti-war and feminist causes. She established the Jane Fonda

Center for Adolescent Reproductive Health in Atlanta, Georgia, in 2001.

Dame Tanni Grey-Thompson, Baroness Grey-Thompson

Paralympic athlete and sports television presenter. She holds 16 Paralympic medals and 30 world records and was awarded a DBE in 2005 for services to sport. Now retired from athletics, she is on the boards of UK Athletics and Transport for London. In 2010, she was made a life peer, and has been the Chancellor of Northumbria University since 2015.

Dagmar Havlová

Humanitarian and former First Lady of the Czech Republic (as the wife of Václav Havel). Founder of the VIZE 97 Foundation, concerned with human rights, youth education, oncology, environmental change and racial intolerance. She is also a member of the philanthropic organization, L'Association Femmes d'Europe.

Swanee Hunt

President of the Hunt Alternatives Fund which has committed some $120,000 to national and global initiatives for social change. She was President Clinton's Ambassador to Austria, and has authored *This Was Not Our War: Bosnian Women Reclaiming the Peace*, *World's Apart: Bosnian Lessons for Global Security*, *Rwandan Women Rising* and the memoir, *Half-Life of a Zealot*. She was inducted into the National Women's Hall of Fame in 2007.

Bianca Jagger

Activist and humanitarian. Jagger works with several human rights organizations, including Amnesty International and Human Rights Watch. She was Chair of the World Future Council from 2007 to 2009, and is President of the Bianca Jagger Human Rights Foundation, as well as Goodwill Ambassador for the Council of Europe.

Nataša Kandić

Human rights activist and founder of the Humanitarian Law Center in Belgrade. She is the organizer of the Candles for Peace Campaign and the Black Ribbon March. Kandić has received more than 20 peace awards for her fight for human rights in Serbia.

Kathy Kelly

Co-coordinator of Voices for Creative Nonviolence, a campaign of resistance to end the Iraq war and the global war on terror. Kelly was also the initiator of Voices in the Wilderness, a campaign to end the UN/US sanctions against Iraq in 1996.

Martha Lane Fox, Baroness Lane Fox

Businesswoman, founder of Lastminute.com. Lane Fox is founder of grant-giving trust Antigone, and has been non-executive director of Marks & Spencer plc, Channel 4 Television and mydeco. She co-founded Lucky Voice Private Karaoke in 2005. In early 2013, she was awarded a CBE and made a life peer shortly afterwards.

Dame Ann Leslie

Award-winning journalist and broadcaster. She has reported from more than 70 countries. She was made a Dame Commander of the British Empire in 2006 for services to journalism.

Professor Wangari Maathai

Environmental and political activist, founder of the Green Belt Movement in Kenya in 1977. She was the first woman in East and Central Africa to earn a PhD and the first African woman to win the Nobel Peace Prize in 2004 for her contribution to sustainable development, democracy and peace. She wrote her memoir, the *New York Times* bestseller, *Unbowed: My Autobiography* as well as *The Green Belt Movement: Sharing the Approach and the Experience*. She died in 2011.

Mairead Maguire

Co-founder of Peace People, an organization set up in 1976 dedicated to peacefully resolving the Troubles in Northern Ireland. She was awarded the Nobel Peace Prize in 1976 and the Pacem in Terris Award in 1990.

Mary McAleese

President of Ireland in 1997, inaugurated as eighth President of Ireland and re-elected 2004. A former journalist, university Professor and Vice-Chancellor, and a former director of Channel 4 Television. She received the American Ireland Fund Humanitarian Award in 2007. She is also a member of the Council of Women World Leaders.

Soledad O'Brien

Journalist and news anchor. Former co-anchor of CNN's *American Morning*, she has appeared as a television anchor and correspondent on MSNBC, CNN, Al Jazeera America and HBO. One of the team who received a Peabody Award for their coverage of Hurricane Katrina, she won the NAACP President's Award in recognition of her humanitarian efforts and journalistic excellence in 2007. Currently, she is the anchor for *Matter of Fact with Soledad O'Brien*.

Sinéad O'Connor

Singer and songwriter. Since she became world-famous with her no.1 hit "Nothing Compares 2 U" in 1990, O'Connor has been an outspoken critic of the oppression of women. Nominated for many awards, she won a Grammy for Best Alternative Music Performance in 1991. Recent albums have included *Theology* (2007), *How About I Be Me (And You Be You)?* (2012) and *I'm Not Bossy, I'm the Boss* (2014). In 2017, O'Connor changed her legal name to Magda Davitt.

Yoko Ono

Avant-garde artist and musician. Her 2001 retrospective "YES YOKO ONO" won the International Association of Art Critics USA Award for Best Museum Show. In 2002 she received the Skowhegan Award for assorted mediums in art, and she was awarded the National Arts Award for Outstanding Contributions to the Arts in 2008. She has been a peace activist and campaigner against racism and sexism since the 1960s.

Mariane Pearl

Journalist and humanitarian. After her husband Daniel Pearl's death at the hands of terrorists in 2002, she wrote her memoir *A Mighty Heart*, which was adapted into a movie starring Angelina Jolie.

Kim Phuc

UNESCO Goodwill Ambassador and peace campaigner. Often called "the girl in the picture", after she was photographed as a child running naked in the street after a napalm attack in the Vietnam War. In 1997 she founded the Kim Phuc Foundation International, to help children who are victims of war from all over the world.

Paloma Picasso

French and Spanish fashion designer and businesswoman, best known for her jewellery designs for Tiffany & Co and her signature perfumes. She is the youngest daughter of 20th-century artist Pablo Picasso and painter and writer Françoise Gilot.

Sister Helen Prejean, CSJ

American advocate for the abolition of the death penalty. Acted as spiritual adviser to several inmates on Death Row and wrote the autobiographical account of her experiences, *Dead Man Walking*, published in 1993, which formed the basis of a feature film starring Susan Sarandon, as well as an operatic adaptation. She is the author of *The Death of Innocents: An Eyewitness Account of Wrongful Executions* and is presently at work on her spiritual memoir, *River of Fire: The Spiritual Path to Death Row*. She is the recipient of several awards including the Pacem in Terris Award and the World Methodist Peace Award.

Dame Paula Rego

Artist. Rego confronts issues such as gender inequality and abortion in her work. She was a Turner Prize nominee 1989, and received an honorary doctorate from Oxford University in 2005. She was made a Dame of the British Empire in 2010.

Louise Ridley

Award-winning journalist. Formerly special projects editor at HuffPost UK and news editor for BuzzFeed UK. Shortlisted for the British Journalism Awards in 2017, and finalist in the Women of the Future Awards 2017, she was also named one of *The Drum*'s 50 Under 30 Women In Digital 2015.

Mary Robinson

First female President of Ireland (1990–97). After her presidency Robinson spent five years as United Nations High Commissioner for Human Rights. She is President of Realizing Rights and one of the Elders brought together by Nelson Mandela. In 2009 she was awarded an honorary degree from the University of Bath; in the same year she was also presented with the Presidential Medal of Freedom by Barack Obama.

Professor Jody Williams

Peace campaigner. Williams spearheaded the Ottawa Treaty, an international treaty outlawing the deployment of landmines. She was awarded the Nobel Peace Prize in 1997.

ACKNOWLEDGMENTS

My gratitude and thanks to Duncan Baird and all at Duncan Baird Publishers.
Also Watkins Publishing for the new edition of this book.

Special thanks to my son Danny for his encouragement and faith in me. It was his concept that inspired me to make this book happen.